The Great
BAMBINO

BABE RUTH'S LIFE IN PICTURES

SAM CHASE

CENTENNIAL BOOKS

The Great
BAMBINO

BABE RUTH'S LIFE IN PICTURES

CONTENTS

Countless words have been written
detailing the life, times and incredible
feats of George Herman "Babe" Ruth Jr.

An American Icon

A larger-than-life figure, Babe Ruth left a legacy that endures today.

While many of today's famous athletes are set up for stardom from a young age, Babe Ruth certainly was not. A troublemaker on the streets of Baltimore who was chewing tobacco and drinking whiskey by the age of 8, young George Herman Ruth Jr. seemed a better candidate for prison than he did for a spot on a professional baseball roster.

His accomplishments far surpassed merely reaching the big leagues. After discovering his talent for baseball at a boarding school for orphans and delinquents, Ruth saw his star rise quickly. While his baseball legacy is largely that of a slugger, Babe's early years in the big leagues were spent primarily as a pitcher. By 1916, his third season with the Boston Red Sox, he posted a minuscule 1.75 ERA across 40 starts. In 38 starts the next season, he threw 35 complete games. He was the best pitcher in baseball, and he was only in his early 20s.

But Babe had a feeling he could also excel at the plate. As he started to take more at-bats, it became clear just how special he was. In 1918, despite having only the sixth-most plate appearances on his own team, he led the entire AL with 11 home runs. The next year, he shattered the single-season home run record with 29. And he was just getting started.

Babe's life and baseball history changed forever on December 26, 1919, when the Red Sox traded him to the New York Yankees. While Boston wouldn't win another World Series for 86 years—blame it on the Curse of the Bambino—the move to the Big Apple launched Ruth into true superstardom.

On the diamond, he won the Yankees their first-ever championship and several more after that, forming the centerpiece of one of the greatest lineups in the history of the game. He broke his own home run record, broke it again, and broke it a third time with 60 bombs in 1927. By the time he retired, there were few significant batting records that he did not own, and several still bear his name today.

In his public life, he blossomed from a naïve young ballplayer into a bona fide A-list celebrity. He was the toast of New York, a fun-loving partier who'd gallivant with the rich and famous. Still, he never lost touch with the down-home charm that made him so lovable to begin with.

The statistics speak for themselves: seven World Series championships, 2,873 hits, 714 home runs. But when it comes to Babe Ruth, the numbers don't capture what he meant—and still means today.

—*Sam Chase*

1

A TROUBLED YOUTH

Long hours working at their saloon and the tragic deaths of several of their young children left George Ruth and his wife, Kate, little time to look after their son, George Jr. He got into enough trouble as a boy that he was sent away to boarding school at a very young age.

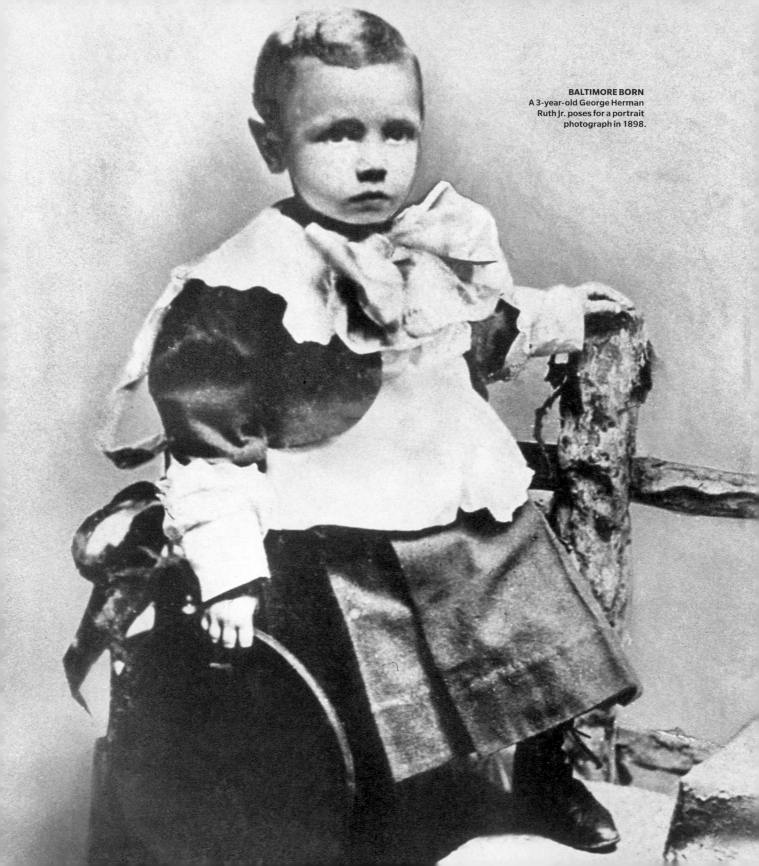

BALTIMORE BORN
A 3-year-old George Herman
Ruth Jr. poses for a portrait
photograph in 1898.

BIRTHPLACE OF A LEGEND
George Jr. was born at 216 Emory Street, a row house located just a few blocks from Baltimore's inner harbor. The house would be converted into the Babe Ruth Museum in 1974.

Every hero has an origin story: the roots and circumstances that shaped who they could ultimately become. For Babe Ruth, a man who became a myth unto himself, it's only fitting that the circumstances of his youth are shrouded with uncertainty. Accounts of his childhood are long on lore, and short on facts.

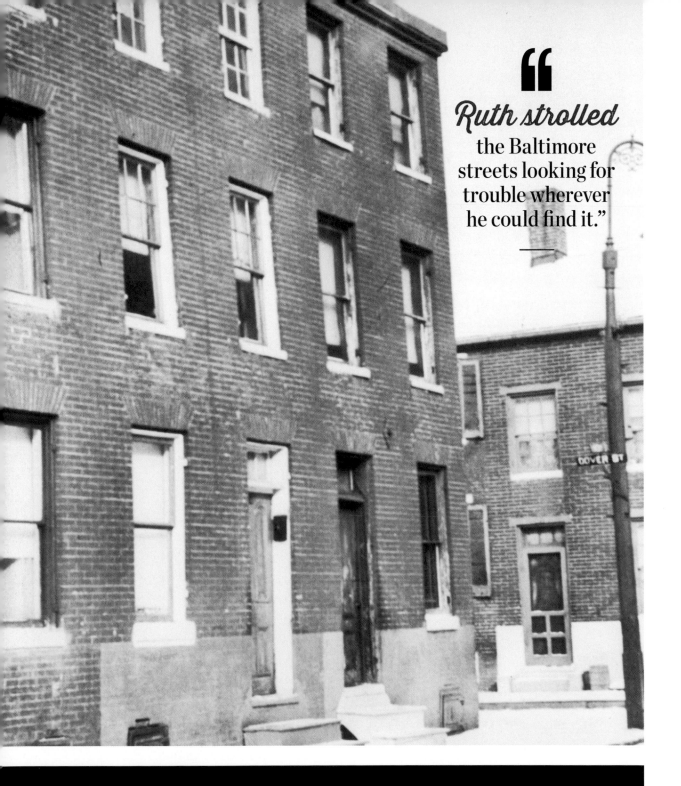

"Ruth strolled the Baltimore streets looking for trouble wherever he could find it."

FAMILY BUSINESS
A 1915 photograph shows George Jr.(second from right) with his father, George Sr. (far right), behind the bar at the saloon. Even after making it as a ballplayer, he would return in the off-season to help run the business. That ended in August 1918 when George Sr. tragically died from injuries he suffered in a brawl outside the bar.

E ven the official birthday of this poor boy from Baltimore who would go on to become one of America's all-time greatest athletes is not known with certainty. For most of his life, he believed he was born on February 7, 1894. That is, until 40 years later, when he requested a birth certificate so he could acquire a passport, and the document he received listed his birthday as February 6, 1895. But the legitimacy of this date, too, must be taken with a grain of salt: Baltimore birth records offer no definitive proof.

What we do know: George Herman Ruth was born the son of George and Catherine "Kate" Schamberger Ruth. Big George, as he was known around the neighborhood (Junior was known as Little George), was the son of a lightning-rod manufacturer, and he dabbled in the same line of work himself while also spending stints as a bartender, horse driver and salesman. The Ruths were of German descent and frequently spoke German around the house, to the extent where George was comfortable breaking into German when called upon in his adult years.

Kate suffered from much illness and heartbreak: Of her eight children, only George and his younger sister Mamie survived through infancy. When Little George was 6, Big George opened a saloon and moved his family into the apartment above it. Both Big George and Kate spent their waking hours managing the bar to make ends meet, so they barely had time for Little George. He was left to his own devices.

By no account was young George Ruth considered to be particularly mean or malicious, but he

"*When Ruth* was 6, his father opened a saloon and moved his family into the apartment above."

At the strict St. Mary's Industrial School for Boys, where many students struggled with behavioral issues, baseball was a healthy way for them to channel their energy. In the back row is a 17-year-old George Ruth Jr., who towered over many of his younger classmates.

was inarguably mischievous and misbehaved. He strolled the Baltimore streets looking for trouble wherever he could find it, lobbing eggs at truck drivers, stealing from shopkeepers and indulging in alcohol and chewing tobacco. Mind you, this was not a troubled teenager, but instead a child who hadn't yet reached the age of 9.

Given his behavior, Little George avoided school whenever he could. Looking back, experts believe he likely suffered from attention-deficit/hyperactivity disorder, and his aversion to educational settings meant that he could neither read nor write. Realizing that Little George was headed down the wrong path, George and Kate made the decision in June of 1902 to send their young son to live and study at St. Mary's Industrial School for Boys.

Located 4 miles from the Ruth family home in Baltimore, St. Mary's was part industrial training school, part reform school and part orphanage. After a prompt 6 o'clock wake-up, students got dressed, attended Mass and ate breakfast, all before the opening school bell at 7:30. From there, the boys were in class until late afternoon, save for a quick lunch break. After class, they had an hour of outdoors time for recreation before dinner. Students were in bed in their dormitories by 8 p.m. There was little deviation from this routine. It was a special occasion indeed when a St. Mary's student was permitted to venture outside the gates that marked the school's perimeter.

St. Mary's maintained a student population of roughly 800 boys ranging from ages 7 to 21, so George Jr. was among the youngest at the school when he moved in from across town. But despite being loud and outspoken, he became popular among teachers as well as fellow students. In his older years, he would become something of an older brother to younger, undersized students, often offering them candy he had bought from the school store. He also developed discipline, at least in some small measure—he grew to enjoy the industrial aspects of his education, and he became proficient at such tasks as rolling cigars and sewing together shirts. He also learned to read and write.

Like most boys at the strict school, Ruth's favorite parts of the day were the free outdoor period between classes and supper. It was there that he found his first mentor, a man known to the Xaverians as Brother Matthias. A giant of a human being, Matthias would tower over Ruth, who was large for his age. Known for his fairness and warmth, Matthias was the favored father of many St. Mary's students despite his role as school disciplinarian. He took Ruth under his wing.

In these recess sessions, Matthias introduced Ruth and other new students to the game of baseball. He would practice with them by hitting long fly balls for the students to field, sending baseballs rocketing through the air with smooth, one-armed swings. "I think I was born as a hitter the first day I ever saw him hit a baseball," Ruth later said.

Baseball was so popular among the student body at St. Mary's that more than 40 teams existed within the school to accommodate players of all ages and skills. Ruth emerged as a star in his teen years, rising to prominence in the school as one of the rarest of diamond oddities: a left-handed catcher. Equipped with a catching glove built for righties, he would catch the ball in his left hand,

tuck the glove into his right armpit, and pull his left hand out of the glove to return the ball to the pitcher—or to gun down a runner at second base with a laser throw.

His big arm had coaches quickly ushering him to the mound, where Ruth was just as dominant

> **In his first** full season in a St. Mary's league, George Jr. homered in nearly every game and never lost a game as pitcher."

as he was at the plate. In his first full season in a St. Mary's league, he homered in nearly every game and never lost a game as pitcher. He became so good that the school let him leave, at the age of 19, on weekends during the summer of 1913 to play semipro baseball locally, an exceptional privilege at the insular academy. Brother Matthias and the rest of the staff at St. Mary's knew they had a remarkable talent on their hands. No one, however, could have imagined just how far he would go. ◆

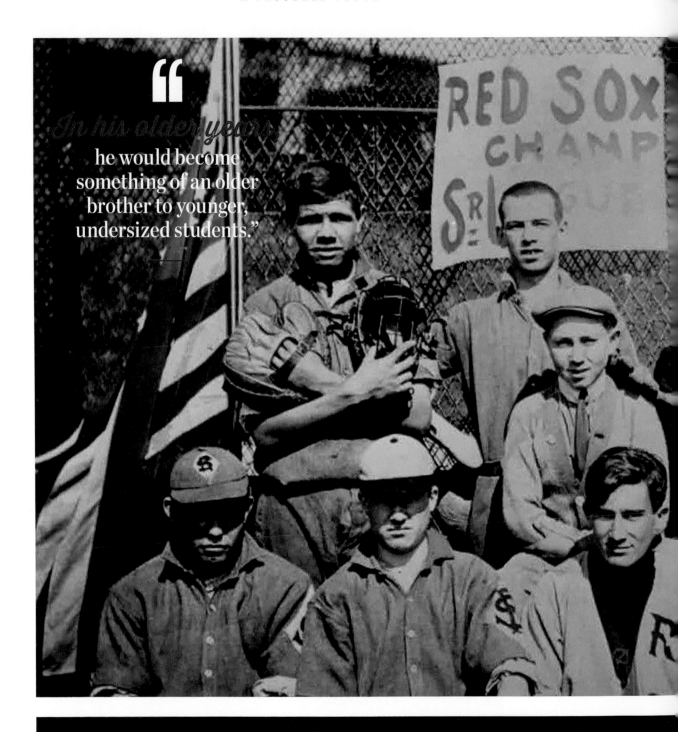

" *In his older years,* he would become something of an older brother to younger, undersized students."

Ruth, top left, posing with his teammates at St . Mary's in an old photo. The promising prospect left in 1914 at age 19 to play minor league ball.

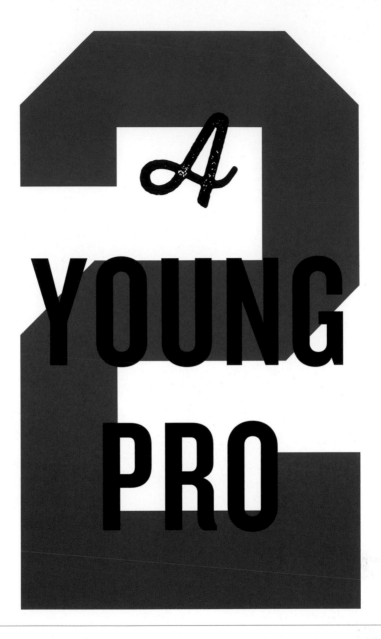

CHAPTER

A YOUNG PRO

Pro baseball represented a different lifestyle for Ruth, who had barely left Baltimore's borders in the first 18 years of his life. Initially signed to a local minor league team, that change accelerated when he was dealt to Boston just months into his first professional season.

MAJOR MINOR
It didn't take long for Babe to go from the big leagues back to the minors, but he soon made an impact on the roster of Boston's Independent League affiliate, the Providence Grays.

WARMING UP
Babe was inserted into Boston's starting rotation after star Red Sox hurler Carl Mays suffered an injury early in the 1915 season. He took full advantage of the opportunity, posting an 18–8 record that year.

Jack Dunn was a well-liked professional baseball player, and a pretty good one at that. By the time he had inhabited the clubhouse role of savvy veteran for the New York Giants in what would be his final season playing in the majors, he knew he wanted to go on to manage a ballclub of his own.

He got the chance soon after, when in 1909, his former manager Ned Hanlon sold him the Baltimore Orioles of the minor Independent League. Dunn couldn't afford a big league team, and he enjoyed scouting local amateur leagues for prospects.

In the spring of 1913, one such scouting trip brought him to St. Mary's Industrial School for Boys to watch George Ruth Jr., whose feats on the diamond had become well-known throughout Baltimore. It wasn't until the baseball off-season, though, when Dunn came back to sign the prospect who would go on to become one of the greatest athletes in history. He returned the following February and, after watching Ruth throw for 30 minutes, was satisfied that the young pitcher would fit in with his Orioles. It was Valentine's Day 1914 when Dunn signed Ruth to a $600 contract for the upcoming season. After two more weeks at St. Mary's and a weekend spent at his father's house, he embarked for spring training.

His older, wiser teammates immediately seized on his naïveté. On his first train ride with the team to spring training, he was convinced to sleep overnight with his left arm in a small hammock intended for luggage so as to "rest" it. Predictably, he woke up with a sore pitching arm. Once in Fayetteville, North Carolina, seemingly each new day brought a new revelation for the provincial fireballer. Upon being exposed to new food options and learning that he could expense meals to the team, his legendary appetite was unleashed.

Ruth became obsessed with the hotel elevator, riding it repeatedly from the lobby to the top floor and back again. He had trouble ingratiating himself to his new teammates—not least of all because

SAME OLD KID IN TOWN
Babe was the center of attention during his brief stint with
the minor league Orioles. But while he drew strong interest
from Baltimore newspapers because he was born and
raised locally, crowds were more often drawn to the
crosstown Baltimore Terrapins of the Federal League.

he couldn't seem to remember their names—so he befriended local youths and borrowed their bikes to get around Fayetteville. For his all-around cherubic nature and his status as Jack Dunn's star prospect, he earned the nickname "Dunnie's Babe." Soon he was just Babe, and before long he was hardly called anything else.

While Babe had quickly earned a reputation as a goofball off the field, no one laughed at the 6-foot-2 pitcher when he was on the baseball diamond. He was the No. 2 starter for Dunn's Orioles, a team that featured an exceptional amount of talent for a

> ## *Upon learning*
> that he could expense meals to the team, the rookie's legendary appetite was unleashed."

minor league outfit. After escaping a bases-loaded jam in the first inning, Babe cruised in his first career regular season start, going the full nine innings for a six-hit shutout—and added a couple of base hits for good measure—in a 6–0 Baltimore win. There was just one problem: The Orioles set a franchise record for low attendance in that game with fewer than 200 fans, as the crosstown Baltimore Terrapins of the Federal League had drawn away many supporters. With revenue from gate receipts declining, Dunn had to dump contracts to stay afloat.

"

Babe had
a girlfriend in Boston before he even had a locker at Fenway Park."

———

For minor league teams at this time, selling top prospects to big league teams was an integral part of their business models. On Thursday, July 10, 1914, Dunn sold Babe, Ernie Shore and Ben Egan to the Boston Red Sox of the American League, meaning Babe was headed to the majors.

Babe was in his new city for mere minutes before he had his first meaningful encounter. After arriving at Boston's Back Bay Station by train, Babe, along with Shore and Egan, dropped their bags off at their hotel before patronizing a coffee shop. There, Babe flirted with the waitress, a pretty 16-year-old named Helen Woodford. The two hit it off immediately, and Babe came back to the coffee shop each morning thereafter for several days to advance his courtship. He had a Boston girlfriend before he even had a locker in Fenway Park. He would marry Woodford before the season reached its close.

That same day, July 11, he made his debut with the Red Sox. After reporting to manager Joe Carrigan's team later that morning, Babe started on the mound for the Sox against the Cleveland Indians. He pitched seven full innings and picked up a win in a back-and-forth 4–3 victory. But Carrigan's trust would not last through Babe's rookie

ROOKIE SEASON
The 1914 *Baltimore News* Babe Ruth baseball card features the young pitcher playing for the minor league Baltimore Orioles. One version of the card sold at auction in 2013 for $450,300.

RUTH
PITCHER

INTERNATIONAL
LEAGUE BALTO.

"

In his first season with Boston, Babe was frequently benched."

year. After getting yanked in the fourth inning of his second start, he went weeks without seeing any action in non-exhibition games. There were a variety of possible explanations for his benching, ranging from the Red Sox's already deep roster to a rumored habit of tipping his curveballs to batters by sticking out his tongue. Another reason may have been the same immature behavior that made him the subject of hazing by older players in Baltimore. Despite being a 20-year-old rookie pitcher, Babe insisted on getting regular time in the batting cage at practice. The habit so irked his veteran teammates that they once cut all of Babe's bats in half with a saw. He ended up playing the stretch run of the 1914 season for the Providence Grays, Boston's Independent League affiliate.

In 1915, Babe became a key member of the major league club. Despite a 1–4 start, he finished 18–8 on the mound for the year, and the Red Sox turned blistering hot in the latter half of the summer to win the pennant at 101–50. Babe wasn't the only star on the staff: Rube Foster, Dutch Leonard, Smoky Joe Wood and Ernie Shore, who arrived with Babe from Baltimore, all won at least 15 games. Plus, Carl Mays became widely regarded as the best reliever in baseball. But when the World Series against the Philadelphia Phillies finally came around, Babe hardly took the field. Carrigan had more faith in his more established veteran starters, and the only action Babe saw in the series was a pinch-hit groundout in Game 1. The Sox would end up winning the World Series in five games, but for Babe, the 1915 season represented unfinished business. ◆

Rise IN BOSTON

3

Once he had settled in to the life of a ballplayer, Babe found himself on the fast track to stardom in Boston. It would be only a couple of years before he became the best pitcher in baseball—and a couple more after that before he would emerge as the game's top hitter.

DAUNTING ON THE MOUND
Babe established himself as an
elite starting pitcher in 1916,
leading the American League
with a career-best 1.75 ERA.

GOING THE DISTANCE
While it was far more common for a pitcher to throw a complete game in Babe's era than it is today, he was still a workhorse by 1917 standards, leading the American League with 35 complete games that season.

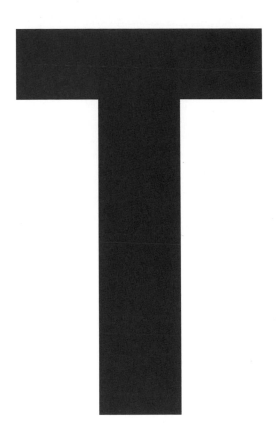

There were some worries that the Red Sox wouldn't be able to compete at the same level in 1916. Babe's weight had ballooned to above 210 pounds, although it would quickly become clear that his paunch wouldn't affect his performance at the plate or his dominance on the pitching mound.

More concerning were the contract disputes that cost the team both Smoky Joe Wood and center fielder Tris Speaker, who had won the MVP in 1912 and was a Boston icon. A slow start to the season seemed to confirm the concerns, especially when the remaining members of the pitching staff failed to live up to the high standards they'd set in 1915.

The one exception was Babe—he was even better. He had arguably the best season of any pitcher in the league, in fact, leading the American League with a 1.75 ERA and nine shutouts, and finishing with a 23–12 record in a league-high 40 starts.

For baseball fans across the country, an exciting new rivalry emerged in the 1916 season—one between the young Babe and Washington Senators hurler Walter Johnson. Nicknamed "The Big Train" by legendary sports writer Grantland Rice, Johnson was the American League's unquestioned top dog on the mound throughout the 1910s—while 1916 would be Babe's first 20-win season, it would be Johnson's seventh 25-win season. Babe and The Big Train squared off four times that year, with Babe winning three of the four duels. While all four games were exciting, the one that really stood out took place at Fenway Park on August 15. Each starter pitched into the 13th inning of that game before Boston ultimately broke through with a run against Johnson to earn a 1–0 victory.

Babe kept the Red Sox afloat during a rocky first half of the season, and a resurgence from his teammates helped the team win the American League with 91 victories. When the World Series came around, Babe got his chance to be a postseason hero. His Game 2 start against the Brooklyn Dodgers would go down as one of the

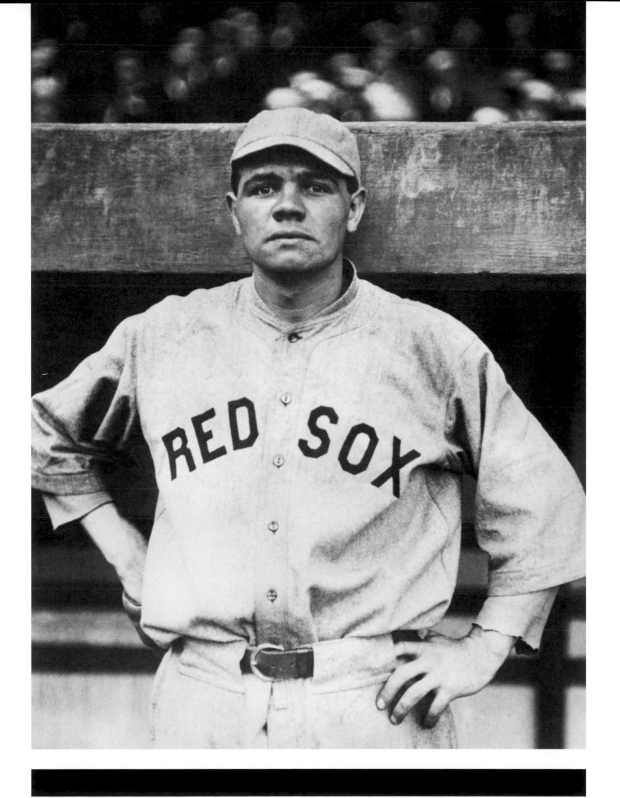

YOUNG AND IN LOVE
Helen Woodford was only 17 years old when she married Babe in October 1914. The couple bought a house in Sudbury, Massachusetts—where, it is rumored, Babe once heaved a piano—quite possibly the one pictured here—into a lake.

"

Legendary pitcher Walter Johnson and Ruth maintained a rivalry throughout the 1916 season, with Ruth notching 23 wins and Johnson 25."

greatest games in baseball history, as he pitched 14 full innings in a back-and-forth battle, ultimately coming away with a 2–1 win. It remains today the most innings ever pitched in a World Series game, and the Sox went on to win their second consecutive championship, again in five games.

While Babe's season-long heroics certainly helped ingratiate him to his older teammates, he was still often the butt of a joke when goofing around with the guys. He insisted on joining his teammates' poker games despite seeming to barely know the rules, losing his money every time and smiling all the while. He also went to great lengths to join a clubhouse barbershop quartet, a pastime that was actually a popular trend with ballplayers at the time. He earned plenty of cheers with his audition song of "Molly, My Dear," but the a cappella council still rejected him, jokingly claiming

FEARSOME FIVE
Boston starting pitchers (from left) Rube Foster, Carl Mays, Ernie Shore, Babe and Dutch Leonard (pictured here during the 1915 season) won a combined 89 games in 1916.

CHIEF RIVAL
Babe warms up for a game against the Yankees
at the Polo Grounds early in the 1917 season.
Five of his career-high 24 wins that year would
come against New York, as he threw a complete-
game victory each time he faced the Yankees.

that the young pitcher's still-changing voice would cause problems for the group's harmonies.

The world was a different place when the 1917 season began, as Woodrow Wilson had declared war on Germany five days prior to opening day. When the Sox opened the season at the Polo Grounds against the Yankees, both teams marched in drill formation—a practice that had been mandated

> **"**
> *Babe was*
> the best pitcher in the American League in 1916, leading with a 1.75 ERA and nine shutouts."

beginning in spring training. Boston started hot and so did Babe, who was 10–1 as a starter as the month of May came to a close. But with each passing week, talk of a military draft grew louder. One finally took place in June for all men between the ages of 21 and 30, and the Sox—along with every other team in the league—lost some players as a result. Babe, however, was exempt because of his marriage.

As a bona fide star in the league, the usually good-natured Babe began to develop the surly

on-field attitude that many great athletes flash at one time or another. An extreme and, ultimately, historic incident of that attitude took place on June 23 at Fenway Park. After walking a batter on four straight questionable balls to start the game, Babe charged umpire Brick Owens, grazing him with a punch as he was restrained by teammates. He was not only ejected, but also escorted off the field by a police officer. Ernie Shore came out to replace him and retired the next 26 batters he faced, making Babe part of the first combined no-hitter in baseball history. Only Babe's walk in the one at-bat he pitched kept it from being a perfect game.

Babe would finish the year with a 24–13 record, representing his career high for wins in a season, and a 2.01 ERA. Boston, however, finished nine games behind the pennant-winning White Sox. Boston was hurt even more than its opponents by departures to the military, and they struggled to overcome injuries to Shore and other key players.

> **"**
> *The usually*
> good-natured Babe began
> to develop the surly attitude
> that many great athletes
> flash at one time or another."
> ———

Plus, it was a legendary White Sox team to which they finished second, one that featured many of the same players who would become part of the infamous Black Sox scandal two years later. The campaign did end on a personal high note for Babe, who pitched five scoreless innings in a charity All-Star Game against some of the league's best sluggers.

As his career as a pitcher progressed, Babe found himself growing increasingly comfortable at the plate as a big leaguer. He saw limited at-bats as a starting pitcher batting in the No. 9 slot, but his maligned insistence on giving himself batting practice reps appeared to be paying off: He batted .325 in 123 at-bats in 1917, and he had seven career home runs through that year. Most impressive was the distance of those homers; when Babe got a hold of one, he really got a hold of one. And as a Boston lineup depleted by the draft struggled to produce, it became clear that a team with a hitter like Babe on the roster couldn't afford to put him up to bat only once every fourth or fifth game.

On May 6, 1918, one day after hitting a home run as a pitcher, Babe got his first-ever start in the field as a first baseman at the Polo Grounds. He homered again. The next afternoon in Washington, he homered for a third straight game. This was no small feat: Only six members of the Red Sox hit a single home run at all in 1918, and Babe was the only one to hit more than one. An illness sidelined Babe in the middle of the month, but he came back to blast four homers over a four-game stretch upon his return. By the end of May, the decision had been made: Babe Ruth—one of the best pitchers in all of baseball—would be moved off the mound to focus on his hitting.

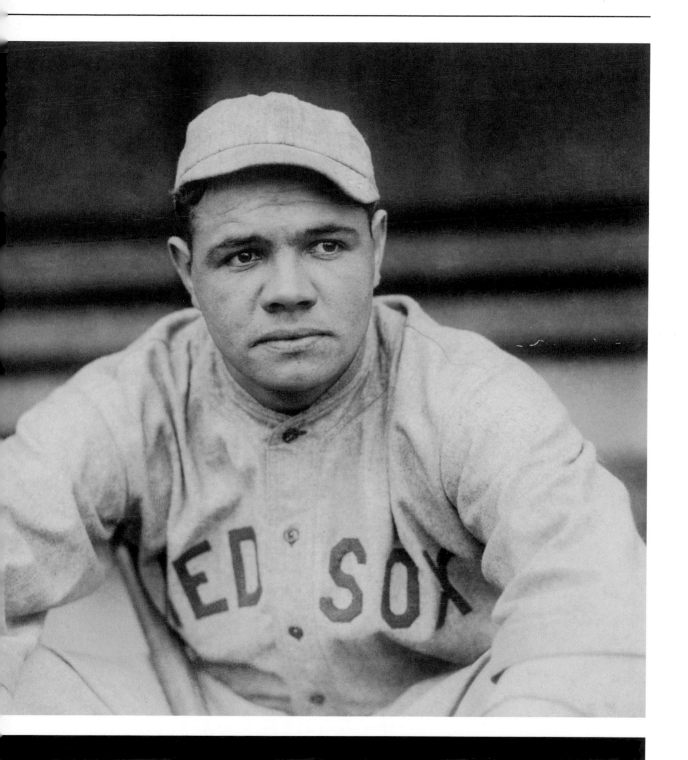

FAST FACT *N°1*

1918 SLUGGING PERCENTAGE

.555

Babe wasn't merely adequate at the plate when he first began to transition from pitcher to hitter; he quickly emerged as baseball's best. He led the American League in slugging percentage in 1918, and his .690 career mark remains the best in the history of baseball.

The rest of the season was tumultuous. Manager Ed Barrow was the member of the organization who was least keen on moving Babe into the lineup—a now-obvious misjudgment in Barrow's outstanding management career—and he accused Babe of slacking off when he refused to pitch at the same steady rate as before. Things came to a head on July 1 in Washington, when a blowout fight between Babe and Barrow in the dugout caused Babe to skip town for Baltimore while the Sox headed to Philadelphia. Babe said he was going to abandon Boston to start playing for a ballclub in a league comprised of shipbuilders along the Delaware River, a threat taken seriously enough to be reported in newspapers. But he was sheepish and contrite when a Red Sox representative finally caught up with him in Baltimore, and he returned to the team to work things out with Barrow.

The efforts of the war caused fans to turn on the game of baseball a bit, and the World Series was nearly canceled. While it ultimately was not, the season was shortened, and the Sox won the American League at 75–51 to set up a World Series meeting with the Chicago Cubs. Needing all the help they could get, Boston started Babe as a pitcher in Game 1 and was rewarded with a 1–0 victory. After sitting the next two games—Barrow was all in again on Babe's pitching, it seemed—he pitched Boston to a 3–2 win in Game 4 at home to give the Sox a 3–1 series lead. The Sox lost Game 5 but won Game 6, the latter in which Babe played briefly as a pinch hitter. Boston won a World Series that nearly didn't happen, and it was a good thing, too—because they wouldn't win another one for 86 years. ◆

Deal of
THE
CENTURY

With Babe Ruth's star on the rise and Boston's profits plummeting, something had to give. The result was the most infamous transaction in baseball history, and the ensuing hex that would plague Beantown for more than eight decades: The Curse of the Bambino.

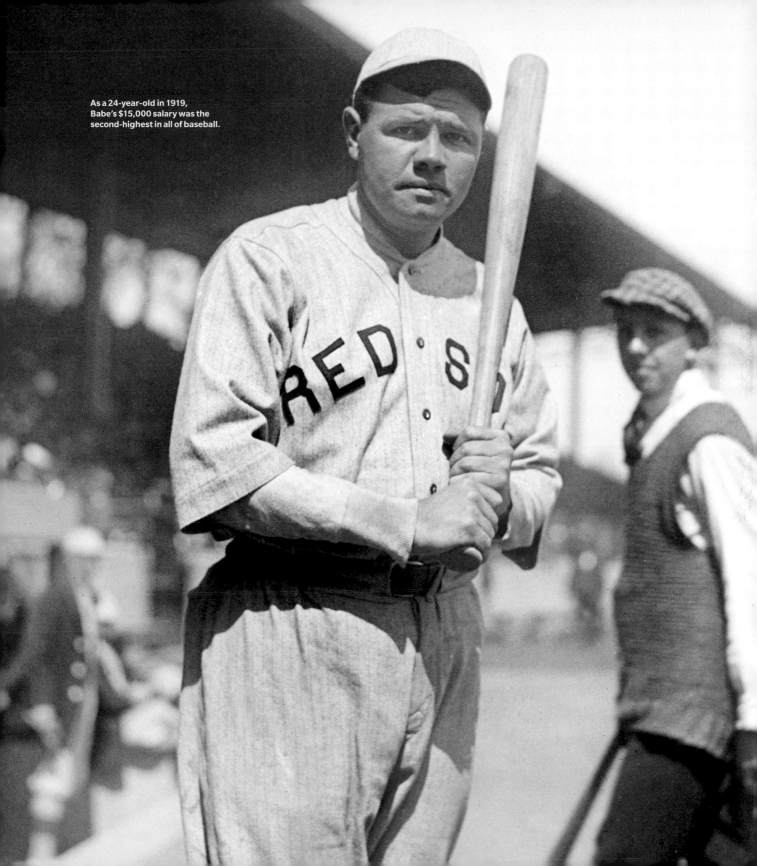

As a 24-year-old in 1919, Babe's $15,000 salary was the second-highest in all of baseball.

TWO-WAY WONDER
Babe was a force as both a batter and pitcher in 1919, which would turn out to be his final season in Boston. He led the majors with 29 homers, and on the mound he posted a solid 2.97 ERA over 17 appearances.

With the war ending two months after the 1918 World Series, which was Boston's third championship in Babe's four full years with the team, the star player felt he was ready to negotiate a new contract with the Red Sox. He asked for $15,000 per year for two years, considered an enormous raise from the already substantial $7,000 that the player was pulling in annually.

Only Ty Cobb, entering his 16th year in the majors, was making more money in baseball. For Red Sox owner Harry Frazee, who had purchased the team from Joe Lannin after the 1916 season, this represented a significant financial burden. Primarily due to the war, gate receipts at Fenway Park had fallen 35 percent in 1918, and that was down from another tough year the season prior. At the same time, Babe was easily his biggest draw for getting fans in the seats, and losing him to a holdout or a rival team could make a bad situation even worse between the Red Sox and its fans. Frazee and Babe agreed on a three-year, $10,000 per year, contract.

B abe was happy with the money, but he had one more wish he wanted accommodated alongside his new deal: He wanted to be completely done with pitching, and play every day as a left fielder. Frazee made sure Barrow assented, but it likely didn't take much arm-twisting: It was quickly becoming clear that the slugger's bat was unlike anything the sport had seen before. On April 4, 1919, in the first spring training game of the year—played at what was then Plant Field in Tampa, Florida— Babe cranked the longest home run of his career (587 feet), a feat that is commemorated with a plaque that can still be seen today outside the University of Tampa's business school.

The Red Sox would struggle out of the gate, losing game after game thanks to injuries to (and declining performances from) many of the stars that had won them a title just a few months

---

FAST FACT №2

BABE RUTH'S 1919 HOME RUN TOTAL

29

Babe alone accounted for a whopping 6 percent of the 447 homers hit by all American and National Leaguers in 1919. In 2019, no entire team accounted for even 5 percent of major league baseball's home runs.

PRESEASON LAUGHS
From right: Babe and Billy Sunday—a former player turned evangelist—look amused while Red Sox manager Ed Barrow does not during 1919 spring training. Barrow would go on to become manager of the 1920s Yankees teams for which Babe starred.

DONE DEAL
The 1919 contract shipping Ruth to New York was formalized by Yankees owner Jacob Ruppert and Red Sox owner Harry Frazee. A January 5, 1920, editorial in *The New York Times* warned a precedent was being set that larger markets would be the ones to garner the best talent.

prior. Things were so bad that Babe reluctantly agreed to pitch a few games to try and lift the squad back to .500, but he didn't pitch particularly well. His bat, on the other hand, awoke after he'd batted just .180 for the first month of the season, and he was back up to .325 by mid-June. With the fans taking interest in Babe—and little else—at Fenway Park that season, Barrow decided to move him off the mound and solely into the lineup. On July 5 against the Philadelphia Athletics at Fenway Park, Babe hit two home runs in a game for the first time in his career. By July 12, thanks to homers in back-to-back games in St. Louis and then Chicago, he had matched his 1918 total of 11 home runs. He hit nine in that month alone, and by July 29 he had already tied the American League record of 16—with 53 games still remaining on the schedule.

After a two-week drought in which fans and reporters waited for the record-breaking 17th,

In 1919,
Babe hit a home run in every American League ballpark, smashing the home run record."

Babe delivered on August 14 and caught fire immediately thereafter. Home run No. 28 came late in August on the longest shot in the history of the Polo Grounds. During the ensuing weekend in Washington, D.C., the last of the season, he hit his 29th and final homer of the year. It was his first at Washington's Griffith Stadium in 1919, and it gave him the distinction of having hit a home run in every American League ballpark that year. Babe had smashed the home run record in the most emphatic way possible.

Babe had become the biggest star in American sports, and he began to act like it. Johnny Igoe, his agent, sent him to Los Angeles for a postseason tour that included exhibition games, charity golf appearances—his drive off the tee was as booming as one might expect—and photo shoots. Frazee even joined in for a publicity picture, posing as the master from Oliver Twist with a bowl of porridge while Babe jokingly pleaded, "Please, sir, I want some more." Everyone was riding high off the big guy's momentous season.

In private, Babe was asking for more—and was hardly begging. He wanted his salary doubled to $20,000, and Frazee knew he deserved it. The slugger had been a few gusts of wind away from doubling the American League home run record, and his outsize persona made him baseball's biggest draw. A postwar resurgence in the sport's popularity meant team owners could no longer cry poverty.

But Frazee, by all accounts, was in dire financial straits. A New Yorker who owned theaters,

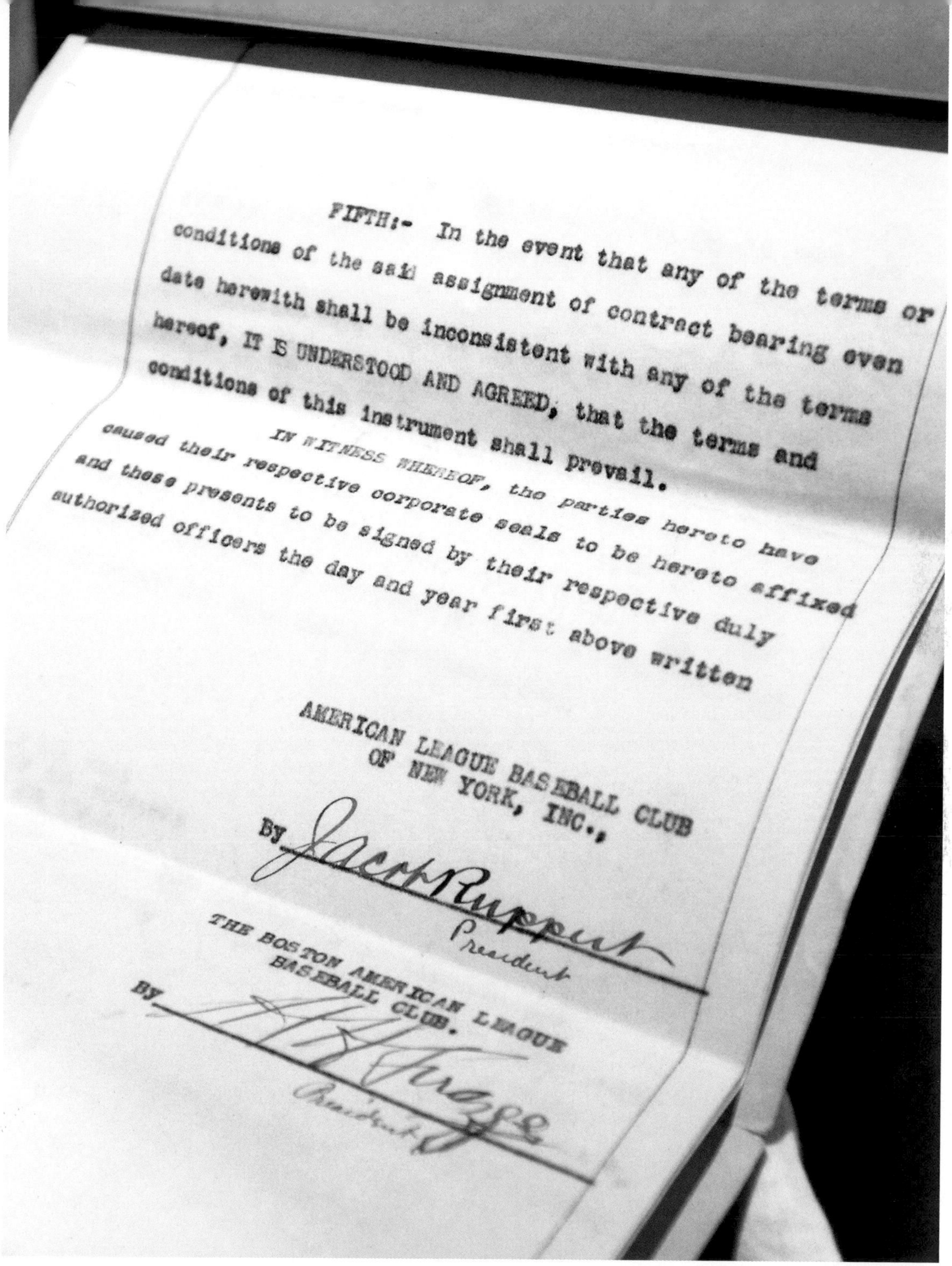

FIFTH:- In the event that any of the terms or conditions of the said assignment of contract bearing even date herewith shall be inconsistent with any of the terms hereof, IT E UNDERSTOOD AND AGREED, that the terms and conditions of this instrument shall prevail.

IN WITNESS WHEREOF, the parties hereto have caused their respective corporate seals to be hereto affixed and these presents to be signed by their respective duly authorized officers the day and year first above written

AMERICAN LEAGUE BASEBALL CLUB
OF NEW YORK, INC.,

BY *Jacob Ruppert*
President

THE BOSTON AMERICAN LEAGUE
BASEBALL CLUB.

BY *H. H. Frazee*
President

> ❝
> *A deal was struck*
> to sell Babe to the
> Yankees straight-up
> for $100,000, double
> the amount of the
> previous largest sum
> ever paid to acquire
> a baseball player.❞

and produced and directed many of the plays they featured, he had bought a Red Sox franchise in 1916 that was the most successful—and one of the most valuable—in baseball at the time. Along with his theater partner Hugh Ward, Frazee bought the club from Joseph Lannin for a total of $1 million. It was a complicated arrangement: $662,000 for the team, $400,000 of which was paid in cash up front and $262,000 of which was committed to a three-year payment plan. Then there was a $188,000 mortgage for Fenway Park that Frazee took on, effectively becoming the owner of the stadium. Another $150,000 issued in preferred stock brought the total to $1 million.

Frazee borrowed his share of the $400,000 that would be paid in cash to Lannin, adding to

debt he already owned in the name of various theater ventures around the country. Once the 1917 season began, his first as owner, he must have quickly realized he was in trouble. Attendance at Fenway fell from 496,397 in 1916 to 387,856 in the 1917 season, and further still to 249,513 in the war-shortened 1918 campaign. Although it bounced back up to 417,291 amid the league-wide 1919 attendance resurgence, the boost at Fenway Park was not as great as it was at some of the other ballparks around the league. With recurring debt payments of $50,000 and a payroll featuring some of baseball's biggest—and highest-paid—stars, Frazee was approaching financial ruin with each passing month.

In the middle of the 1919 season, star pitcher Carl Mays grew so frustrated with the team's struggles and, from his perspective, mismanagement, that he left the team in the middle of a game in Chicago, flew back to Boston, and declared his time with the club to be over. Yankees president Jacob Ruppert and his extravagantly named business partner Colonel Tillinghast L'Hommedieu Huston moved to acquire Mays from the Red Sox in exchange for a role player and, more importantly to Frazee, $40,000 in cash.

After the year, Frazee resolved to sell Babe. While it was an enormous decision, it was not a difficult one for the cash-strapped owner. He once again reached out to the duo of Ruppert and Huston, and found that the Yankees owners were indeed eager to bring in the biggest headlining attraction in all of baseball. They had plans to

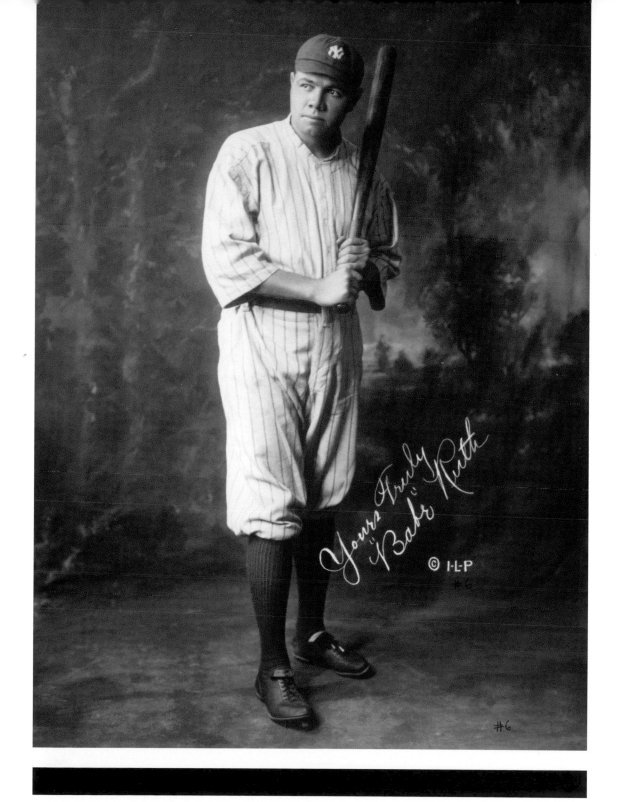

Yours Truly "Babe Ruth"

© I·L·P

#6

#6

> ## *The decision*
> to sell Ruth was not a difficult one for the cash-strapped Red Sox owner."

open a new stadium in the years to come, and they needed a franchise centerpiece to attract fans to the ballpark. A deal was struck to sell Babe to the Yankees straight-up for $100,000, double the size of the previous largest sum ever paid to acquire a baseball player. Frazee was desperate for even more money, though, and the deal came to include a $300,000 loan tendered to him by Ruppert, an arrangement that oddly made the Yankees owner the indirect proprietor of Fenway Park.

Yankees manager Miller Huggins flew to California to deliver the news in person, and found his new player on a golf course. If Babe experienced disappointment, he didn't show much of it—he quickly turned the conversation to his contract situation. While his salary remained the same, he was promised bonuses that would bring his Yankees income to $41,000 for the next two seasons, surpassing the sum he had unsuccessfully demanded in Boston. ◆

Home
RUN
KING

Only one American city was big and bright enough to contain Babe's enormous personality: New York. From the moment he arrived, it was clear that the Bambino and the Big Apple were a match made in heaven.

BOW DOWN
After Babe smashed the home run record yet again with 59 in 1921, Yankees manager Miller Huggins bestowed him with this silver crown in the Polo Grounds clubhouse and declared him "The Sultan of Swat."

Babe Ruth entered his prime at an opportune moment in the history of baseball. As fans flocked back to the game after the war, team owners did everything they could to show them a good time. This consisted, primarily, of propping up teams' offenses.

The spitball was banned in both leagues at the turn of the '20s, with the exception of existing spitballers who were grandfathered in and allowed to throw the pitch for the remainder of their careers. Furthermore, rising American wool prices in the aftermath of the war compelled the league to switch to baseballs made with Australian wool, which happened to be springier. Baseballs traveled farther upon impact.

Still, Babe remained far ahead of the pack, even as hitters around the league saw their statistics begin to balloon. By July 15 of his inaugural season with the Yankees in 1920, he had matched his already monumental home run record of 29 from the previous year. In the second game of a doubleheader that same day, he hit his 30th and 31st. He would end up hitting 54 home runs that year, destroying his own record. No other *team* in the American League topped 50, and no other player reached even 20. Babe's .847 slugging percentage that season became his most enduring record, lasting 81 seasons until Barry Bonds topped it in 2001. (Ruth remains baseball's career slugging percentage leader at .690.) The Yankees would end up finishing third in the American League.

The next season, in 1921, "The Sultan of Swat" was somehow even better. On July 18, he hit his 26th homer of the year. Landing an estimated 580 feet from home plate at Detroit's Navin Field, it was easily his longest measured homer to date. It was later determined that it was also special in another way: At 139 career home runs, Babe had topped Roger Connor's record of 138 that had stood since 1897. In a late-season series that would determine the winner of the American League

HOME FIELD ADVANTAGE
While the Polo Grounds was never
considered a hitter's park, *every* park was
a hitter's park for Babe: He launched
85 home runs there despite the fact that
it was his home park for only two seasons.

"

The Giants

were not a crosstown
rival; they also played in
the Polo Grounds. It was
the first time the entire
World Series was played
at a single site."

pennant, the Yankees hosted a highly anticipated
four-game set against the Indians. The Yanks took
three of four, thanks in large part to Babe's 57th
and 58th home runs of the season. He finished
with 59, and the Yankees won the pennant.

The ensuing World Series matchup was a fas-
cinating one: The Yankees versus the New York
Giants. The Giants weren't a crosstown rival;
they also played in the Polo Grounds. It was the
first time the entire World Series was played at
a single site. The showdown was also intriguing
for the team's sharply contrasting styles. While
Babe and the free-swinging Yankees represented
the extreme cutting edge of baseball's offensive
revolution, legendary manager John McGraw's
Giants were the most staunch holdouts of the

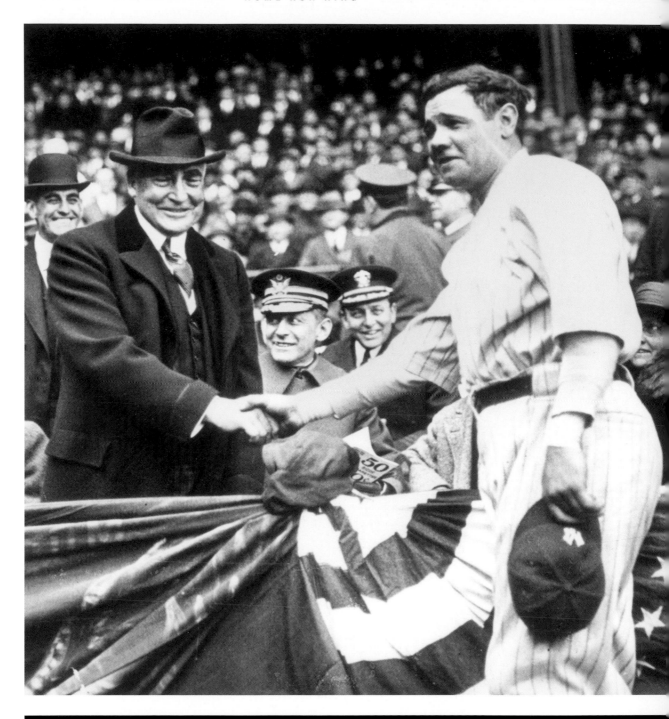

FAST FACT № 3

PREVIOUS HOME RUN RECORD

138

Roger Connor was baseball's all-time leader in home runs until Ruth hit his 139th on July 18, 1921. Connor's record had stood for 23 years, but Babe would ultimately break it more than five times over with his 714 career home runs.

dead-ball era strategies that emphasized walks, bunts and steals—commonly referred to now as small ball. Ultimately, McGraw's Giants won the championship, five games to three, in the fourth and final best-five-out-of-nine World Series ever played. A swollen, infected elbow kept Babe out of three games in the series, decimating the Yankees' chances after they had jumped out to a 2–0 series lead after two games.

When the off-season rolled around, Babe prepared to head out on a barnstorming tour, an activity that had earned him substantial income in years past. (For more on his barnstorming days, see page 74.) A 1911 rule prohibited World Series participants from taking part in such tours, but Babe had flouted the restriction after his 1916 championship appearance with the Red Sox to little consequence. But this time around, Kennesaw Mountain Landis was in charge. The federal judge had been named baseball's first-ever high commissioner a year earlier—meaning he was in charge of both the American and National Leagues—and the disciplinarian by trade had little tolerance for rule-breaking. Knowing this, Babe went on tour anyway. Landis suspended him for the first six weeks of the 1922 season.

When he returned to the Polo Grounds in May, Babe was greeted with boos. The suspension hadn't helped his popularity, nor had a new $52,000 salary that was three times that of anyone else on the roster. Six games into his delayed season, things got worse. He received an ejection when he flung a fistful of dirt into an umpire's face, after which he jumped into the stands to challenge a fan to a fight. "I didn't mean to hit the umpire with the dirt," Babe said after the incident, "but I did mean to hit that bastard in the stands."

> ""
> *The 1923 opening*
> of the $2.5 million Yankee Stadium, directly across the Harlem River from the Polo Grounds, was a fresh start for Babe and the team."
> ___

Babe finished the year with a .315 batting average, down more than 60 points from the season before. He launched 35 homers in 110 games, and the league-wide surge in power meant he finished only third in the league in home runs that season. Despite the relative down year for Babe, the Yanks once again met McGraw's Giants for an all-New York World Series. The Giants triumphed for a second consecutive year, sweeping Babe's team with four straight victories in the best-of-seven series. He managed only two hits in 17 at-bats, a fitting end to a disappointing campaign.

The opening of Yankee Stadium served as a fresh start at the beginning of the subsequent 1923 season. Two years earlier, McGraw, part owner of the Polo Ground–controlling Giants, had told Huston and Ruppert they needed to find a new home for their team. The pair responded by building a majestic $2.5 million stadium directly across the Harlem River from the Polo Grounds. The construction of Yankee Stadium stood alongside the acquisition of Ruth as the foremost accomplishments in the duo's substantial legacy.

While the announced attendance on opening day was 74,217, Yankees general manager Ed Barrow would later admit that the actual attendance was closer to 60,000. Regardless, Babe rewarded them with a three-run blast, the first home run in Yankee Stadium history. It was a blissful start to a blissful year. Babe batted a career-best .393 and won his only Most Valuable Player Award. (The award was first introduced in 1922; players were not allowed to win more than once until 1931. If not for these restrictions, Babe surely would have won several more.) With 41 home runs, he once again led the league. The Yankees won the American League pennant by 16 games, which granted them a third straight shot at beating the Giants for a World Series title. The Yanks won in six games, closing the series in the ballpark that McGraw had forced them to vacate. Babe opened the deciding game with a first-inning home run, his third dinger of the series. Babe had finally won a title for his new team.

Babe remained hot the following season. He won his first and only batting title with a .378 average in 1924, and was easily the home run king, with 46. The lefty slugged so many balls beyond the Yankee Stadium fences that the park's right field bleachers came to be known as Ruthville. The team, however, finished second in the American League, and an aging roster raised concerns about the club's competitive viability going forward. Also raising alarms was Babe's behavior: His notorious off-the-field antics had only worsened in the wake of winning the championship.

Babe showed up to 1925 spring training weighing nearly 260 pounds, 50 pounds heavier than what was considered his ideal playing weight. Once there, he made little effort to get in shape—in fact, he was partying noticeably hard, even by his legendary standards. He fainted more than once during the team's travels through the South. On a return train to New York, he collapsed and cracked his head on the floor. He was checked into St. Vincent's Hospital, where doctors diagnosed him with an intestinal abscess, aka an ulcer. After an operation, Babe remained in the hospital until May 26, more than 30 games into the Yankees' season. When he returned to the club to train, New York sat in seventh place. His ailment became known as "the bellyache heard 'round the world."

After a couple of months of hitting poorly, Babe looked like he was back to his old self in August. Unfortunately, that was true of him in all respects— mere weeks after his multimonth hospital stint, he was back to his old eating, drinking and philandering ways. Yankees manager Miller Huggins had had enough: He suspended Babe indefinitely and fined him $5,000—a figure that, at the time, was greater than most ballplayers' annual salaries. As

> **"**
> *Babe's ailment*
> became known as
> 'the bellyache heard
> 'round the world.'"

the brightest star in baseball, Babe had successfully bullied his way out of more than one suspension over the years. He knew the team could not succeed without him. But in 1925 the team couldn't seem to succeed with him, either, and Huggins decided that now was the time to teach the slugger a lesson. It took an apology to the entire team—something previously considered unthinkable—for Babe to get himself back in the lineup in September. The Yankees would finish the season with a record of 69–85, which landed them in seventh place, a whopping 30 games behind the Senators. It would be the only season between 1917 and 1933 that Babe—who finished with a .290 average, 25 home runs and 66 runs batted in—failed to bat at least .300. ◆

BABE'S
Barnstorming
DAYS

6

Whether it was to make some extra cash or just to bask in the adoration of his fans, Babe Ruth enjoyed the off-season games away from the major leagues just as much as the crowds loved seeing him play.

In the early days of baseball, much of the sport's growth in popularity throughout the United States can be attributed to barnstorming. Beginning in the 1860s, the term was used to describe informally assembled teams which traveled to different towns to play exhibitions.

Originally, these took place primarily only during the time of year and in regions where it was warm enough to play the game. By the 1880s, as leagues better established themselves, barnstorming largely became a postseason activity. In a time before radio and television broadcasts, it was a chance for rural fans to experience high-level baseball and see their local boys take at-bats against the pros. For working ballplayers, it was a relatively easy means of earning extra money in the days long before million-dollar contracts.

In his first exhibition game after the 1915 season (his first full year in the majors), Babe pitched in his hometown of Baltimore. He struck out seven batters in three innings before his catcher became injured. With no backups to pull from the depths of the 25-man roster, Babe switched positions and played catcher himself the rest of the game. What's more, the left-hander had to use a catcher's glove made for righties. He held up fine behind the plate—and in front of it, too, hitting a double in a 4–0 loss. It was a testament to the differences between professional games and barnstorming exhibitions as much as to Babe's seemingly unlimited skills as a player.

Several days later, Babe played another game in Baltimore, this one at St. Mary's Industrial School for Boys, his alma mater. He struck out 14 on the mound and earned two hits in a 12–2 victory. "Babe Ruth Is Hero of Hour. Band Plays in His Honor and Former Associates Cheer," read the next day's *Baltimore Sun* headline. But while he was well-paid for his appearance, away from the field he wasn't so lucky: A diamond ring, which he

TOGETHER AGAIN
A 1927 postseason
barnstorming tour featured
Ruth's Bustin' Babes against
Lou Gehrig's Larrupin' Lous.

" *Residents who* saw top players in their own towns had memories that would last a lifetime."

had bought for $500 from his World Series bonus with the Red Sox (the equivalent of over $10,000 today) somehow disappeared from his belongings.

Often, barnstorming appearances were organized by businessmen who were as eager to hobnob with ballplayers as they were to profit from ticket sales. In October 1916, Ed Maynard of New Hampshire baseball glove manufacturer Draper-Maynard Co. invited Ruth and some other Red Sox players to an exhibition in Laconia. About 2,500 people attended the contest, but the game was just a small part of the itinerary. The players received the key to the city and made appearances in several other Granite State locales before spending the night at Maynard's lakefront estate, along with family and friends who'd accompanied them on the trip. The getaway included a bear hunt, a dinner of steak and suckling pig, and wrestling matches and tango dancing late into the night.

For players who barnstormed every fall, the small towns likely began to blur together after a few weeks. But for the residents of those locales,

seeing baseball's biggest stars up close—on their own local diamonds—formed memories that would last a lifetime. A 1919 trip to Maine saw Babe take on an 18-year-old pitcher named Del Bissonette, locally known as "the Babe Ruth of Maine." The fact that Ruth already inspired such monikers spoke to the size of his emerging superstardom. On the same trip, someone had printed a song about Babe and was selling copies in the stands—another tribute to his near-mythological status.

B abe was nearly as eager to interact with his fans as they were to meet him. He would dedicate long stretches of time to signing autographs after his exhibition games, since many of those fans would never have the opportunity to see him play in Boston, New York or another big league city. Occasionally, attendees got more than just autographs: During a May 1921 visit to Mount St. Mary's College in Maryland, near where Babe grew up, he put on a hitting demonstration for students and locals. What started as a one-man home run derby turned into an interactive clinic, with Babe hitting sky-high fly balls for attendees and even letting the pitcher strike him out, much to the crowd's delight.

While the exhibition contests were lighthearted affairs, some of the games that Babe chose to play sent a broader message. Throughout his career and for about 15 years after it, baseball, like the rest of America, was racially segregated. And while barnstorming was just an off-season gig for the white players of the major leagues, it was more often a full-time job for the Black players of that

> **"**
> *Babe would* spend long stretches of time signing autographs and greeting his fans."

era—and not an especially stable one. Legendary pitcher Satchel Paige claimed to have played for 250 teams in his career.

Babe regularly played barnstorming games against Black ballclubs, sometimes even in regions where mixed-race competition was illegal. He would socialize with Black opponents before and after games, and with Black fans in the stands. On a 1927 visit to play the Kansas City Monarchs, one of the Negro Leagues' most prestigious teams, he hosted 50 orphaned children from the Guardian Angel Home for Negroes at the ballgame.

"The way he lived his life, it's fair to say that he was the first effective proponent for the integration of baseball," baseball historian Bill Jenkinson told the *Baltimore Sun*. "He was enormously influential, and he went out of his way to demonstrate to the white power structure of major league baseball that this is what should be done."

Toward the end of his career, Babe's profile had grown so large that he was not only considered an ambassador for baseball, but also one for the

TAKING THE FIELD TOGETHER
More than 30 years before Jackie Robinson broke baseball's color barrier in 1947, integrated barnstorming teams like the Kansas City All Nations featured Black, white, Japanese, Native American and Latin American players.

country. In 1934, legendary Athletics owner and manager Connie Mack assembled an All-Star team for a barnstorming trip to Japan, with Ruth as the centerpiece. The roster included decorated American Leaguers such as Lou Gehrig, Jimmie Foxx and Lefty Gomez as well as star catcher Moe Berg, who would go on to become an American spy in World War II. Some believe the trip was his first mission.

The Americans left by ship from Vancouver, Canada, and arrived to a scene of chaos in the Port of Yokohama. More than 30,000 fans showed up to greet the ballplayers, causing a massive jam of bicycles and rickshaws in the streets. Turnout for the actual games was no less intense, with 200,000 fans attending the first four contests. When the team practiced 20 miles outside of Tokyo, fans traveled from the city to watch. Even poor weather couldn't put a damper on the proceedings—while playing through a downpour, Ruth fielded balls at first base with one hand and held an umbrella in the other.

The Americans were endlessly wined and dined, giving Ruth ample opportunity to exercise his famous appetite. "We went to one luncheon after another, one dinner after another," recalled Ruth's daughter Julia, who joined in on the trip along with her mother, Claire. "Daddy didn't like the sushi, but he loved the teriyaki—beef, chicken, pork, lobster."

No matter where he toured, whether small-town USA or big-city Japan, Ruth was bound to draw loving fans. As long as his playing days went on, he kept touring—and he loved his fans just as much as they adored him. ◆

7

A MARRIAGE NEGLECTED

It was a shock to no one that Babe Ruth's erratic, irresponsible behavior led to an erosion of his home life—one that ultimately resulted in estrangement, but never divorce. Having lost contact with his wife, the slugger was stunned when he learned that she had tragically died.

A SECRET BIRTH
Babe and Helen offered conflicting responses when asked about the birth of their daughter Dorothy, causing some to speculate that the child had been adopted.

TOO FAR APART
Babe and Helen, shown here in 1923, often seemed happy when they were together. But due to Babe's travel and status as a New York City celebrity, they spent far more time apart from each other.

Babe's off-the-field exploits did not escape the notice of his wife, Helen. His antics were well-documented in the press and the cities in which he played. At his level of stardom, his behavior would have been widely noticed even if he had tried to hide it—and he didn't.

Babe's life in 1914 was very different than what it would become in the years to follow. Given his restrictive upbringing, his courtship of Helen Woodford likely represented his first real contact with a woman. Three months into their relationship, he proposed marriage to her at the same coffee shop in which they met. The betrothed couple took the train to Baltimore, and they wed in St. Paul's Catholic Church in Ellicott City, a community near Baltimore. Because he had not yet turned 21, Babe received a signed certificate from his father permitting the ceremony, and George Sr. housed the newlyweds for the winter in his apartment above the saloon. (Babe's mother had passed away several years earlier.)

Babe and Helen spent the next winter in Baltimore, too. Babe had earned enough money to buy his father a new bar at the corner of Lombard and Eutaw streets, only two blocks from where the Orioles play at Camden Yards today. (The building is now home to a "gentleman's club" known as The Goddess.) Once again, Babe worked the counter, and he and Helen lived upstairs.

Soon, though, their annual off-season began to lose its charm. While Helen could easily turn a blind eye to Babe's philandering ways when he was on the road with the ballclub, she had no choice but to come face-to-face with it when he couldn't tone it down during the winters he spent with her. In October 1917, before the couple had even made the trek down to Maryland, Babe wrecked his car in a late-night Boston accident. He came away unharmed, but an unidentified female passenger was hospitalized. Helen was obviously distraught, but what could she do?

DADDY'S GIRL
Shown here outside his home
in Sudbury, Massachusetts,
Babe maintained a loving
relationship with his daughter
Dorothy for the duration of his life.

"
Helen's alienation
from her husband
heightened when he was
sold to the Yankees."

She cut ties with her family when she wed Babe, and she had little life outside of her relationship with him. She had nowhere to go, a circumstance that would resign her to putting up with increasingly upsetting behavior from her husband.

Nearly a year later, as the Red Sox closed in on clinching the pennant en route to their 1918 World Series victory, tragedy struck at home. One late August Saturday night in the tavern, George Sr. found himself breaking up a fight between various members of his second wife's family. The fight carried to outside the bar, where George was knocked to the sidewalk. His head struck the pavement, knocking him out. He was taken to a hospital and pronounced dead soon after. When Babe and Helen attended the wake the following week, it was the last time either of them would spend extended time in Baltimore. With one fewer anchor in his life, Babe was cast further adrift.

WEDDING BELLS
Babe married his second wife, Claire Merritt Hodgson, on the morning of what was supposed to have been opening day of the 1929 baseball season at Yankee Stadium. (Rain, however, canceled the game.)

GOOD LUCK KISS
After giving his new bride a smooch on the actual opening day, Babe hit his first home run of the season in his very first at-bat.

Helen's alienation from her husband heightened when he was sold to the Yankees. While she found the glamorous lifestyle that Babe sought out in Boston to be unappealing, she was at least in the city in which she grew up. After Babe became a Yankee, the couple moved into a suite in the Ansonia Hotel on Broadway in Manhattan, which represented an existence far removed from Helen's upbringing in South Boston. As he had in Beantown, Babe lived a life largely separate from his wife. And when she was included in his exploits, it became clear why she was more often excluded: A late-night car crash outside Philadelphia on a July off-day in the 1920 season sent both of them flying to the side of the road. He seemed to have as little regard for her well-being as he did his own.

A strange incident during Babe's ill-fated 1922 season highlighted the oddity of his domestic life.

SETTLING DOWN
Shown here hunting quail with Claire in Maine the day before Thanksgiving in 1933, Babe would end up treating his second marriage with much greater reverence than he did his first.

At the tail end of the regular season, reporters spotted Helen pushing a 16-month-old in a stroller around the Ruths' residence at the Ansonia. When asked, she claimed the child was her own, and that it had been hidden from public view due to health issues. Reports emerged that Helen had undergone a series of miscarriages over the years, lending credence to the idea that she may have wanted to keep the birth of a child private. Asked about it by the press, Babe offered vague information, and a birth date for the child that didn't line up with what Helen said. Years later, it became public knowledge that the child, named Dorothy, was Babe's illegitimate daughter with a mistress. Some believed that Babe deceived Helen into adopting her.

By 1925, the situation reached a head. Years of barely hidden infidelity by her husband had taken its toll on Helen. A woman from Long Island, New York, filed a $50,000 paternity suit against Babe, and even though it ultimately fell

> **"*While he clearly* had little regard for his marriage, Babe refused to divorce his wife on principle."**

through, Helen felt especially hurt. Babe was growing sick of the marriage, too—while Helen's protestations served as little check on his gallivanting, he was tired of having to hear them at all. Around the same time Babe was hospitalized early in the 1925 season, the couple split, and Helen headed home to Massachusetts. The distressing situation had caused her to fall ill, too.

Babe had also met somebody else. Unlike Helen, Claire Merritt Hodgson was cosmopolitan and sophisticated. Babe wasn't the first ballplayer she had met, and she wasn't taken with his celebrity in the way that other women were. She didn't immediately sleep with him, either, an act that stood out as unusual and drew further intrigue from the slugger. He quickly fell head over heels, but the relationship remained informal. Despite clearly having little reverence for his marriage, Babe refused to divorce his wife on principle.

Babe and Helen seldom communicated during their estrangement, but he'd occasionally see her for dinner when the Yankees were in Boston. Tragedy struck on a Friday night in January 1929, when Helen was killed in a house fire. The circumstances of her death brought further shock: For two years, she had been living with Dr. Edward H. Kinder, a dentist, and it was his home in Watertown, Massachusetts, in which she perished.

Dr. Kinder sent news of Helen's death to Babe in New York, and he was at a party with Claire on Saturday night by the time he received the call. He cried on the phone upon hearing the news, and

FAMILY MAN
Babe's wife Claire and daughter Julia (far right) join him for Opening Day at the Giants' Polo Grounds in April 1948.

> ❝
> ## *Older and more* mature, Babe had finally reigned in his hedonistic impulses.❞

he boarded a 1:15 a.m. train to get to Boston early Sunday morning. A wake was held that Wednesday night, and a funeral that Thursday.

Three months later, Babe married Claire. The couple had been in a public relationship for years, and he was close with her family. The wedding took place on the morning of what was supposed to have been opening day for the 1929 season at Yankee Stadium. (The game was rained out.) The following day, Claire attended a Yankees game for the first time as Babe Ruth's wife. He homered that day, and the newlywed player blew his wife a kiss as he rounded third base.

Babe's second marriage was far smoother than his first. Older and more mature, he finally reined in the hedonistic impulses that had made him a terrible husband to Helen. Babe and Claire took in Dorothy to raise her alongside Claire's daughter, Julia, who never knew her biological father. The couple remained married until Babe's death in 1948. They are buried next to each other in the Gate of Heaven Cemetery in Hawthorne, New York. ◆

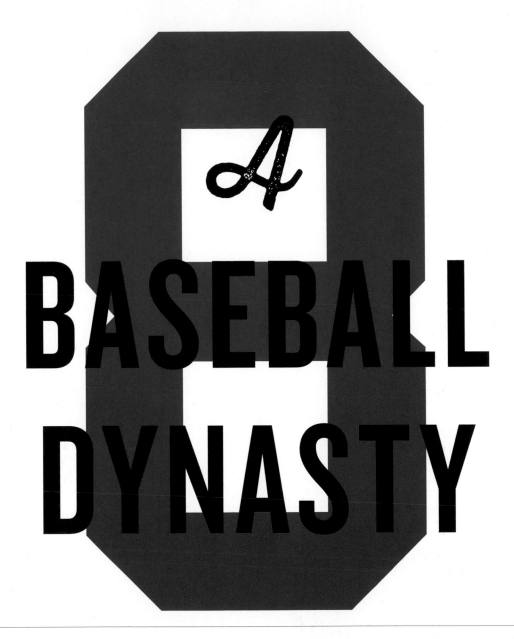

A BASEBALL DYNASTY

After a midcareer crisis derailed his 1925 season, Babe Ruth returned in full force to play the best baseball of his career. And with such stars as Bob Meusel, Tony Lazzeri and Lou Gehrig around him, the Yankees fielded one of the greatest lineups to ever play the game.

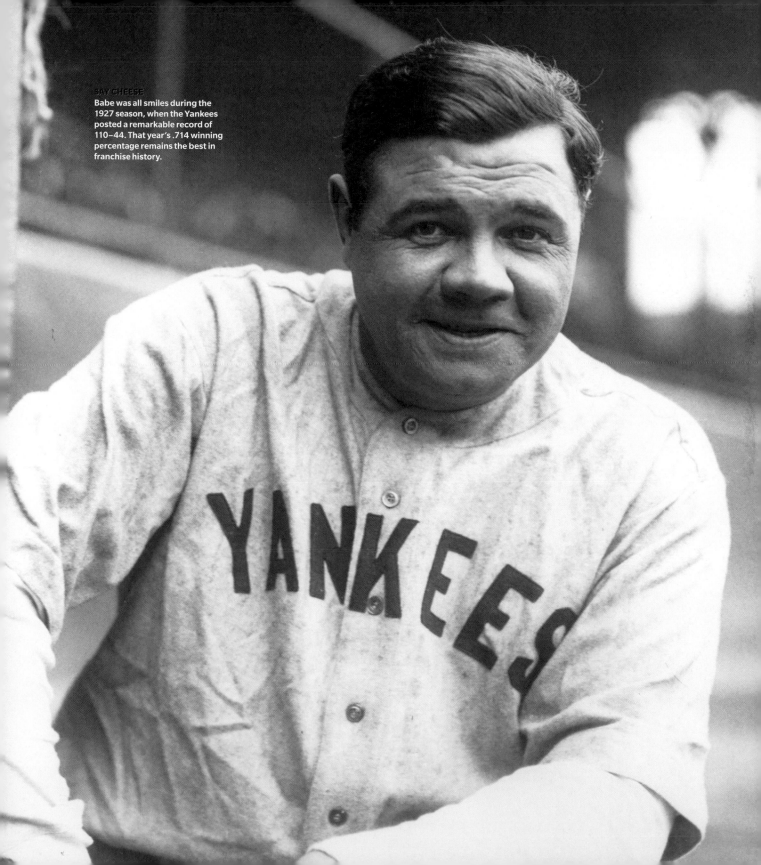

SAY CHEESE
Babe was all smiles during the 1927 season, when the Yankees posted a remarkable record of 110–44. That year's .714 winning percentage remains the best in franchise history.

PUNCH IN THE LINEUP
In an effort to reach peak physical form for the 1926 season, Babe trained at Artie McGovern's famous Madison Avenue gym. Included among McGovern's celebrity clientele were such luminaries as composer John Philip Sousa, boxer Jack Dempsey and golfer Gene Sarazen.

When the dust had settled after the yearlong embarrassment that was the 1925 Yankees season, Ruth showed a renewed commitment to baseball during the ensuing off-season. He skipped what would have been a lucrative barnstorming tour in Canada, turning down an activity from which he had derived enjoyment in prior off-seasons. Instead, he spent the winter in New York and committed to an intense training regimen at a Madison Avenue gym. It was one of the few times in his career that he showed the behavior of a great athlete off the field.

THE STAGE IS SET
Babe led off the fourth inning of Game 3 of the 1926 World Series with a single, one of only five hits the Yankees were able to muster in a 4–0 loss. They would end up losing the series to the St. Louis Cardinals in seven games.

The Yankees entered the 1926 season with reason for optimism, but also several concerns. While their returning talent was far greater than their record from the previous season would indicate, the team's foremost off-season acquisitions, middle infielders Mark Koenig and Tony Lazzeri, were both rookies. A 16-game winning streak to finish out spring training, however, proved to be a valid sign of good things to come; at season's end, the Yanks edged out the Indians to reclaim the American League pennant with a record of 91–63. While hardly a slouch in 1925 when he actually made it onto the field, Babe left no doubt in 1926 as to who was baseball's king at the plate. His 47 homers and 155 runs batted in led the league—with runners-up amassing only 19 and 114, respectively—and he lifted his batting average more than 80 points, from .290 to .372. Add that to a huge rookie year from Lazzeri and an impressive sophomore campaign by first baseman Lou Gehrig, and the New York lineup was something to be feared.

Entering the World Series, the Yankees were the heavy favorites over the 89-win St. Louis Cardinals, and New York won Game 1 by a score of 2–1. Despite his peak physical condition that season, Babe split his pants on a slide into second base, and the game was delayed as a team trainer ran out onto the field to patch things up. Less amusing, though, was when the Yanks lost each of the next two games by a combined score of 10–2. Down two games to one heading into a pivotal Game 4, Babe wasted no time in lifting his team to a lead: He launched the first pitch he saw in the top of the first inning for a

FAST FACT № 4

HOME RUNS FOR RUTH AND GEHRIG IN 1927

107

Babe smashed 60 homers while Lou Gehrig blasted 47 during the 1927 regular season. They became the first pair of teammates to each top 30 home runs, and their combined total remained the highest in one season until Yankee sluggers Roger Maris and Mickey Mantle combined to hit 115 homers in 1961.

MARK KOENIG

BABE RUTH

TONY LAZZERI

BOB MEUSEL

The Yankees of the late 1920s are remembered today as one of the greatest teams in the history of American sports, with a formidable lineup including the six batters known as Murderers' Row.

EARLE COMBS

LOU GEHRIG

EASY STREET
Babe's cheerful demeanor was on full
display when he signed a three-year,
$70,000 contract on March 4, 1927,
a little more than a month prior to the
start of the season.

" *The New York* faithful consistently packed the stadium to its brim as the Yankees chased the pennant.**"**

———

solo home run, then did the same thing in the third frame. The crowd seemed to anticipate that Babe would go deep again when he faced a full count in the sixth inning. He didn't disappoint, blasting a majestic shot past the stadium's confines beyond center field to shatter the windows of a car dealership across the street. It was Babe's first career three-homer game, and the first three-homer game in the history of the World Series.

After splitting the next two games, New York and St. Louis took the field for a series-deciding Game 7 at Yankee Stadium. A third-inning home run from Babe got the Yanks on the scoreboard, but they still trailed 3–2 when Babe worked a walk with two outs and nobody on in the bottom of the ninth. Never one for passive baseball, Babe took off for second on a delayed steal attempt in hopes of getting into scoring position for batter Bob Meusel. Instead, a perfect throw met him at the bag, and Hall of Fame second baseman Rogers Hornsby

tagged him out to end the series. Just like that, the season of redemption had come to an end.

Babe showed no remorse for getting caught stealing (nor for getting caught doing anything else in his life, for that matter). His belief in the process—that the right choice is the one that yields the best chance of success, regardless of whether it ultimately works out—is a philosophy that would be right at home in the analytics-obsessed game of today. More importantly, though, he had a sense that the Yankees' reign was just beginning. He was the only fixture in the Yankees lineup north of 30 years old at 31, and some of the team's brightest talent—namely Gehrig, Lazzeri and Koenig—was under 25.

But even the most enthusiastic optimist could not have predicted just how dominant New York would be in 1927. The nickname "Murderers' Row," first bestowed upon a hot-hitting Yankees lineup two years prior to Babe's arrival, resurfaced to describe the first six batters in the order in '27: Leadoff hitter Earle Combs, followed by Koenig, Ruth, Gehrig, Meusel and Lazzeri, in that order. There were breakout seasons up and down the lineup. Combs and Meusel both posted top-10 American League batting averages, Meusel and Lazzeri ranked among the top 10 in RBIs, and Lazzeri and Koenig formed the best double-play duo in the league. (For more on the famous lineup, see page 110.)

And then there were Babe and Gehrig, who were in a class all their own. Each posted arguably the

RUN BATTED IN
Babe scores on a fourth-inning Bob
Meusel home run in Game 1 of the
1928 World Series. The Yankees swept
the St. Louis Cardinals to win their
second straight championship.

best season of his respective Hall of Fame career,
and Gehrig even led Babe in homers through
mid-August. That was before Babe pulled away
and set yet another record with 60 blasts, the
most he would ever hit. Gehrig blasted 47, nearly
30 more than the third-place Lazzeri, and took
home the league's MVP Award. The Yankees ran
away with the pennant at 110–44, and they swept
the World Series against the Pittsburgh Pirates.
Babe hit two home runs in those four games.

By definition, the one-of-a-kind 1927
season was not replicable, even though
the Yankees returned Murderers' Row
in its entirety. While still elite, the 1928
squad was not nearly as dominant.
Lazzeri and Koenig missed a combined
60 games, a circumstance that opened
a defensive chasm in the middle of the infield
while punching an offensive hole in the middle
of the order. But the one-two punch of Babe and
Gehrig remained formidable, to the point where it
would be hard to imagine any team in the league
losing if it were to acquire the duo. Gehrig's home
run number fell to 27—still good for second-best
in the American League—and he led the league in
on-base percentage and RBIs. Babe hit 54 home
runs, marking the fourth and final time he would
top the half-century mark for homers in a season. It
would be two more years still before someone other
than him replicated the feat, and 33 years before
Roger Maris bested Babe's 60 from the season prior.

If the Yankees or their fans were bored by the
team's success, neither showed it down the stretch.
The New York faithful consistently packed the

SADDLE UP
Ever the ham, Babe roped Gehrig into participating when he played cowboy at the Yankees' celebration of their 1928 World Series sweep over the St. Louis Cardinals.

"

Babe caught
the final out of the series to secure the sixth World Series championship of his career."

stadium as the Yankees chased the pennant. Once they clinched it, Babe bought a piano solely for the team's raucous party at a Detroit hotel. The Yankees advanced to the World Series with 101 wins to face the Cardinals. It was nearly a pattern by now for Babe's Yankees teams, losing a World Series but getting a chance to avenge that loss soon after.

And just as the Yankees ultimately took down the crosstown Giants, they did the same with a four-game sweep of St. Louis. It was a series during which New York rarely trailed, and one that ended with Babe catching the final out in left field to secure his sixth World Series championship. Gehrig dominated St. Louis pitching, batting .545 with four homers and nine RBIs; Babe batted .625 while hitting all three of his homers in a Game 4 clincher. Legend has it that Babe predicted the third homer in banter with pitcher Bill Sherdel before knocking it out of the park. It would not be the last story from Babe's career of a World Series called shot. ◆

The Sluggers of
MURDERERS' ROW

9

Alongside superstars Babe Ruth and Lou Gehrig, the 1920s New York Yankees also fielded one of the greatest lineups in baseball, including Earle Combs, Mark Koenig, Bob Meusel and Tony Lazzeri, who ushered the game into a new era of offensive firepower.

MURDERERS' ROW BATTING ORDER
1. Earle Combs
2. Mark Koenig
3. Babe Ruth
4. Lou Gehrig
5. Bob Meusel
6. Tony Lazzeri

Earle Combs

POSITION: CENTER FIELD

CAREER HIGHLIGHTS
New York Yankees (1924–35)
Career Hits: 1,866
Career Batting Average: .325

f Babe Ruth and Lou Gehrig were thunder, Earle Combs was lightning.

"Up here, we'll call you 'The Waiter,'" Yankees manager Miller Huggins told Combs when he first arrived in the Bronx from his native Kentucky. "When you get on first base, you just wait there for Ruth or Gehrig, or one of the other fellows, to send you the rest of the way around."

From 1924 to 1935, that's exactly what Combs did. He was the consummate leadoff hitter, getting on base with ease and putting his incredible speed to good use once he got there. It's no coincidence that the 1920s Yankees peaked at the same time Combs did—in their historic 1927 season, he posted career bests in batting average (.356), hits (231) and triples (23). League-wide, only Ruth and Gehrig scored more runs than he did that sea-

son. He had a fantastic year the next season, too, finishing sixth in 1928 MVP voting. In addition to his prowess at the plate, he had great range in center field, thanks to his speed.

Combs was a fan favorite. So much so that, incredibly, regulars in the right field bleachers once pooled their money to buy him a gold watch. He was well-respected by his teammates, too, including Babe.

"Combs was more than a grand ballplayer. He was always a first-class gentleman," Ruth once said.

In July 1934, Combs was playing outfield against St. Louis when he crashed into the wall chasing down a fly ball. He sustained serious injuries, including a fractured skull, broken shoulder and injured knee; he was reportedly near death for the first few days and hospitalized for more than two months. He made it back to the field the following season but suffered another major injury—eventually retiring to clear the way for a new rookie center fielder, named Joe DiMaggio.

As for Combs himself, he was the picture of humility, even after winning nine World Series between his playing and coaching days. Upon his induction to the Hall of Fame in 1970, he professed, "I thought the Hall of Fame was for superstars, not just average players like me."

Mark Koenig

POSITION: SHORTSTOP

CAREER HIGHLIGHTS

New York Yankees (1925–30); Detroit Tigers (1930–31); Chicago Cubs (1932–33); Cincinnati Reds (1934); New York Giants (1935–36)

Had a .500 batting average in the 1927 World Series

In his rookie year (1925) he struck out just 37 times in 617 at-bats

While the Murderers' Row is often remembered as a collection of power hitters, Mark Koenig did not fit that mold. While Babe Ruth and Lou Gehrig hit 60 and 47 home runs in 1927, respectively, Koenig launched only 28 in his entire career. But while he didn't have the pop of his more celebrated teammates, the short-stop was nonetheless a key cog in the Yankees' machine of an offense. He hit .285 as a 22-year-old for the '27 Yanks, striking out only 21 times in 568 plate appearances. Plus, he caught fire when it counted, notching nine hits in the World Series sweep over Pittsburgh—three more than Ruth or any other Yankee.

For much of that year, Koenig had a locker next to Babe, slept across from him on team train rides, and took part in his legendary debauchery on road trips. That is, until a dugout fight in Baltimore about an overthrown ball in the infield launched the two into a brief feud.

"We wrestled for a minute or so until the other guys stopped it," Koenig said of the kerfuffle. "I didn't talk to Ruth until we clinched the pennant in St. Louis. We shook hands and it was OK. It was silly."

While Koenig and the rest of the Row are remembered as baseball legends, legacy wasn't something they thought about at the time. "I don't think it entered any of our minds that we were the best ever," Koenig said years later. "We just went on winning."

Bob Meusel

POSITION: LEFT/RIGHT FIELD

CAREER HIGHLIGHTS

New York Yankees (1920–29);
Cincinnati Reds (1930)

Career Home Runs: 156

Career Batting Average: .309

On successful teams, everyone has their role to play, both on and off the field. So it's no surprise that a roster featuring the boisterous Babe Ruth also had its fair share of quiet types. On the 1920s Yankees, none were quieter than "Silent" Bob Meusel. Reporters liked to joke that "hello" and "goodbye" were the extent of a full conversation with the outfielder.

But on the field, where he let his bat do the talking, Meusel was anything but silent. He joined the Yankees as a rookie in 1920 and immediately established himself as an excellent hitter, batting over .310 in each of his first five seasons. Few players were more essential in New York's first-ever championship, as Meusel led the team with eight RBIs in their 1923 World Series victory over the crosstown Giants. In 1925, when Ruth missed a good chunk of the season, Meusel exploded to lead the league with 33 home runs and 134 RBIs. He was second in the AL in steals in 1927, once stealing second, third and home on a single trip around the bases. To this day, he is one of only four players to ever hit for the cycle three times in his career.

While generally soft-spoken, Meusel had his moments of fieriness. In a 1924 game in Detroit, Silent Bob charged the mound after opposing player-manager Ty Cobb instructed his pitcher to throw at him. A fight ensued—not just between the two teams, but also between the hundreds of fans that rushed onto the field. It was Meusel in a nutshell—seldom calling attention to himself, but always in the middle of the fray. The brawl earned him a 10-game suspension and, more importantly, even greater respect from a clubhouse that looked to him for leadership by example.

Tony Lazzeri

POSITION: SECOND BASE

CAREER HIGHLIGHTS

New York Yankees (1926–37); Chicago Cubs (1938); Brooklyn Dodgers (1939); New York Giants (1939)

Five-time World Series champion (1927, 1928, 1932, 1936, 1937)

Batted .293 with 169 home runs during 12 years with the Yankees

Career Home Runs: 178; RBIs: 1,194 Career Batting Average: .292

Late in Game 7 of the 1926 World Series, trailing 3–2 against the St. Louis Cardinals and with the bases loaded, rookie second baseman Tony Lazzeri launched a ball over the fence—just foul. On the next pitch (from future Hall of Famer Grover Cleveland Alexander), he struck out.

It was an iconic moment in baseball history, but hardly one that defines Lazzeri's legacy. The next season, on the much-lauded 1927 team, he hit an impressive .309 with 102 RBIs and 18 home runs, the third-most in the league behind only Ruth and Gehrig. And the following season after that, he upped his average to .332 while finishing third in the MVP race. There was no need for a Game 7 redemption: The Yanks swept the World Series in both 1927 and 1928. Lazzeri accumulated several productive seasons and championships in the years after, and still holds the American League record for RBIs in a single game with 11. He was posthumously inducted into the Hall of Fame in 1991.

A forebear to Joe DiMaggio, Lazzeri also holds a special place in Yankees lore for introducing many Italian American New Yorkers to the game of baseball. To fans of Italian heritage, he was known as "Poosh 'Em Up Tony." Proud to wear the pinstripes, Lazzeri was more than happy to be an ambassador for the ballclub.

"Around New York I used to hear that expression, 'Once a Dodger, always a Dodger,'" Lazzeri said. "But how about, 'Once a Yankee, always a Yankee?' There never was anything better than that. You never get over it."

Lou Gehrig

POSITION: FIRST BASE

CAREER HIGHLIGHTS

New York Yankees (1923–39)

Single-Season RBI Record (AL): 185

Most RBIs Over Three Seasons:
509 (1930–32)

Played in 2,130 consecutive games
(a record held for 56 years)

Bill Dickey once said of his teammate Lou Gehrig, "He went out and did his job every day." It sounds like the least of Gehrig's accomplishments, given how well the man did his job, but it actually may have been his most impressive. He played in a then-unmatched 2,130 consecutive games, a record that was broken by Cal Ripken Jr. in 1995, but otherwise remains unapproached.

Gehrig and Ruth were all-time greats, legends in their own rights, and inextricably linked. Between them, they helped baseball's most decorated franchise win its first six World Series championships, and pushed each other to statistical heights that would have been unimaginable just several years earlier. In some ways, their diverging personalities complemented each other.

"I'm not a headline guy," Gehrig said. "I know that as long as I was following Ruth to the plate I could have stood on my head and no one would have known the difference."

Occasionally, they also clashed. "They didn't get along," Tony Lazzeri once said. "Lou thought Ruth was a bigmouth and Ruth thought Gehrig was cheap. They were both right."

By most accounts, though, the pair maintained a mostly friendly relationship. That is, until around 1932 or 1933, when Gehrig's famously prickly mother reportedly made a comment about how Babe and Claire Ruth dressed their daughters. The incident resulted in a falling out between Babe and Lou, who would barely speak for years.

Fortunately, the two had a brief, but powerful, reconciliation after Gehrig was diagnosed with ALS, the disease that would take his life. At Lou Gehrig Appreciation Day on July 4, 1939, they met with a hug instead of a handshake. Babe, as Gehrig's wife, Eleanor, described him, was "big and bearlike, hugging away the feuds of the past summers."

"

ranked almost as high as, or higher than, Ruth in RBIs, hits and home runs throughout his career."

FOR THE RECORD
Gehrig hit more doubles and triples
and averaged only nine home
runs fewer than Ruth with twice
as many MVP Awards, but he
garnered much less attention
both on and off the field.

10

The CALLED SHOT

Even after the Yankees dynasty of the 1920s drew to a close, Babe Ruth remained the game's most feared slugger. Appearing in his first World Series in four seasons, he hit a breathtaking home run in the 1932 Fall Classic that would live forever in baseball lore.

STILL THE KING
A 36-year-old Babe surveys the scene at Yankee Stadium before taking the field against the Red Sox in May 1931. He would end up leading the American League in home runs that season with 46.

It was a contract year for Babe Ruth in 1929—not that there was any doubt that a payday awaited him on the other side of the season. After the death of his first wife, he spent a quiet off-season with new wife Claire that culminated in their marriage the day before the regular season began.

At 34 years old, Babe showed that he was still baseball's most formidable power hitter. He led the majors in slugging percentage (.697) and homers (46) while batting .345 and knocking in 154 runs. Lou Gehrig finished second in the American League with 35 home runs, and Tony Lazzeri hit a career-high .354 while matching his career-best homer total with 18. The rest of the lineup struggled, however, with Bob Meusel slugging under .400 for the only time in his 11-year career in what would turn out to be his final season in the Bronx. Mark Koenig drove in only 41 runs, which would help facilitate his departure midway through the following season. The Yankees did manage to go 88–66, but they finished 16 games behind a Philadelphia Athletics team led by superstars Al Simmons and Jimmie Foxx.

Any disappointment on the field, however, was dwarfed by the unexpected death of manager Miller Huggins late in the season. Huggins had been coaching ill all year, but it wasn't until September 20 when he finally checked himself into the hospital. Diagnosed with a severe bacterial skin infection, he would pass away five days later. When the ballclub received the news at Fenway Park, where they were playing that afternoon, Babe and the rest of the clubhouse broke down in tears. The team traveled back to New York for the funeral.

When the time came to search for a manager after the season, Babe threw his name into the ring. While it had been several years since he had truly clashed with a manager, he was never one to enjoy answering to authority. Plus, already possessing the respect of the clubhouse as the superstar of the team, it wouldn't take him long

OVER THE WALL
Babe launches one of the two home runs he hit in Game 3 of the 1932 World Series in Chicago. It was in this game that he hit his famous "called shot," silencing a rowdy overflow crowd at Wrigley Field.

" *According to* Gehrig, what Babe said was, 'I'm going to knock the next pitch right down your goddamn throat!'"

to earn trust as a player–coach. But management said no, giving the job instead to former Yankees pitcher Bob Shawkey.

In need of a new contract, Babe decided to leverage the perceived slight and asked Jacob Ruppert for a $100,000 salary. For context, his expiring $70,000 annual agreement was nearly three times that of Gehrig, the next-highest paid player on the club at $25,000 a year. Babe got talked down to $80,000, which meant he still earned more than the $75,000 salary of the President of the United States. When asked about making more money than Herbert Hoover, Babe quipped, "Why not? I had a better year than he did."

Not that it was a high bar, but the Bambino outperformed Hoover in 1930, as well. He hit .359 with a league-best 49 homers and 153 RBIs. But the ballclub once again underperformed. Shawkey was replacing a legend in Huggins, and he failed to gain the respect of some of the more prominent players. (Babe, for one, liked him.) The Yankees fell

FAST FACT *N° 5*

CAREER WORLD SERIES HOME RUNS

15

Babe appeared in 10 World Series, the last seven of those as a Yankee. After homering only once in 44 at-bats over his first five appearances in the Fall Classic, he belted an astounding 14 home runs in 85 at-bats over the five series he played between 1923 and 1932.

to 86 wins, this time finishing third behind Philadelphia and Washington. Shawkey was booted after one season at the helm.

Babe again asked for the job, but a large part of the reason for Shawkey's dismissal was that Yankees ownership had their eyes on another target. Chicago had fired Joe McCarthy, a young but well-respected manager who had brought the Cubs to the World Series in 1929. The team saw him as someone who could be a long-term replacement for the beloved Huggins, who had helmed the team for more than a decade.

The clubhouse dynamic in 1931 was something of a reversal from that of 1930, where this time everyone liked the manager except Babe. "Cleancut" wasn't exactly the slugger's style, but it was the policy that McCarthy instilled for his players— he made them wear jackets and ties on road trips.

For all his bluster, McCarthy stayed out of Babe's way, and in turn, Babe grew to respect him. In his first year with the team, McCarthy got the club back up to 94 wins, a total that in many seasons would have been enough to win the pennant. But the Philadelphia Athletics blew away the rest of the American League at 107–45, and the Yankees were shut out of the World Series for a third straight season. Babe and Gehrig tied for the league lead with 46 homers.

In 1932, New York returned to dominance, posting a 107–47 record to conquer second-place Philadelphia by a 13-game margin and ending a three-year pennant drought. While Babe was starting to slow down at age 37, only by his high standards could a season with a .341 batting average, 41 homers and 137 RBIs be considered a down year. He did, however, surrender the American League home run title for the first time since 1925, as Philadelphia's Foxx nearly matched Babe's single-season record with 58 home runs. However, more concerning than the slight decline in production were Ruth's struggles with injuries. He ruptured a muscle in his leg in July, and a late-season illness threatened to keep him out of the World Series.

But with the twilight of his career clearly nearing, the Fall Classic was not something Babe was going to miss. When McCarthy's old team, the Chicago Cubs, arrived in the Big Apple for Game 1 of the series, a piece of news made its way to the New York locker room: Former Yankee Mark Koenig had been stiffed by his teammates and given only a partial share of the Cubs' collective bonus for having reached the World Series, because he had played only a partial season. With Babe as the boisterous ringleader, the Yankees relentlessly taunted Koenig's new teammates

> **"The called shot stands out as legendary, not just in Babe's career but in the history of sports."**

before, during and after their respective 12–6 and 5–2 wins in Games 1 and 2.

The Cubs were incensed, and so were their fans. Hyped up by the incitement of the Chicago press, the Cubs faithful greeted the slugger with vitriol when he took the field for Game 3. Babe, however, was loving it. Usually a fan favorite even when on the road, he jovially tossed lemons back into the stands after Cubs supporters heaved them in his direction during pregame warmups. After he and Gehrig put on a show with home run after home run in batting practice, each slugger homered within the game's first three innings.

This made Wrigley Field fans even angrier. When Babe stepped up to the plate in the fifth inning of a 4–4 game, the place was a madhouse. Cubs players walked out of their dugout and openly hollered at him for the duration of the at-bat that followed, something that probably ought to have merited umpire intervention. Regardless, Babe was having the time of his life, openly jawing with opposing players outside the Cubs dugout, fans, and catcher Gabby Hartnett and pitcher Charlie Root. After receiving strike one, he raised a single finger in the air. After getting strike two, he raised two fingers. Root shouted something at him, and he shouted back. According to Gehrig, what Babe said was, "I'm going to knock the next pitch right down your goddamn throat!"

He very nearly did, but the ensuing line drive was smoked so hard that it traveled past Root, past the center field fence and deep into the bleachers—

the longest home run in the history of Wrigley Field to that point. The crowd finally hushed, and Babe had something to say to every infielder he passed on his trot around the bases. It's an endless debate as to whether he actually pointed his bat to center field before hitting the blast, as he later claimed in his biography, but there is little doubt that Babe had announced his home run to the crowd before stepping up and hitting it. The called shot stands out as a legendary moment not just in the career of Babe Ruth, but in the history of American sports.

Gehrig hit his second homer of the afternoon on the next pitch, and the Yankees took a 3–0 series lead with a 7–5 win. The next day, they took down a demoralized Chicago team by a 13–6 score to win in a four-game sweep, giving Babe his fourth World Series title as a Yankee. It was the seventh—and would turn out to be the final—championship of his career. ◆

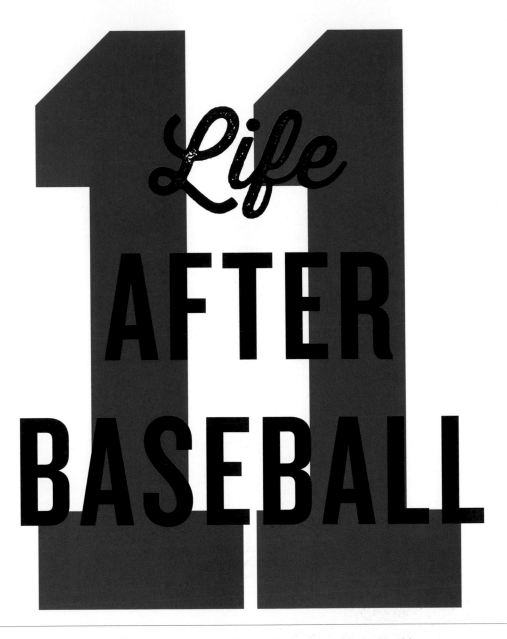

Life

AFTER

BASEBALL

A series of indignities peppered the final seasons of Babe Ruth's career,
after which he turned to golf and little else in retirement. When he passed away
from cancer at the age of 53, tens of thousands of fans gathered to mourn his death.

Dapper and distinguished, Babe loved dressing up and hitting the town during his baseball career. But as his star faded in retirement, he took less pleasure in the public outings that he had once made so frequently.

RETURN TO BOSTON
After having played 15 seasons for the Yankees, Babe spent the final 28 games of his career as a player–coach in 1935 for the National League's Boston Braves.

B

Babe had little leverage when the Yankees cut his salary by a third after the 1932 season. America was in the midst of the Great Depression, and few had sympathy for baseball's highest-paid slugger. It was also becoming clear that his best playing days were behind him.

BIRTHDAY BOY
Celebrating his 47th birthday at his
New York City apartment, Babe
prepares to cut a birthday cake given
to him by "May and Peter," whom
Babe described as "very dear friends."

The club ultimately let him save some small amount of face by agreeing to negotiate up to a $52,000 salary from their $50,000 offer. For Babe, fresh off his World Series heroics, it would be the first in a series of indignities that would pepper the remainder of his career in baseball.

The Yankees slipped a bit in 1933, and the same was true of Babe. The team finished second in the American League, and Babe ranked second in the league with 34 home runs, trailing far behind Jimmie Foxx's 48. While his batting average (.301) and RBI total (104) were also solid, they were lower than in any of his prior seasons as a Yankee, aside from his injury-marred 1925 campaign. The highlight of the season came at major league baseball's first All-Star Game, which was played at Chicago's Comiskey Park. Babe was slotted into the starting lineup for mostly sentimental reasons, and in the third inning he launched a two-run home run—the first home run in All-Star Game history. He also pitched for the final time in his career in the final game of the regular season, helping his own cause with a decisive homer in a 6–5 Yankees victory. He finished with a 94–46 career record on the mound with a 2.28 ERA.

The following off-season brought another substantial pay cut, this time down to $35,000 a year. Making less than half of what he had two years earlier, he still had the biggest salary in the game. He once again told Yankees brass that he wanted Joe McCarthy out and would like to be manager himself, but, no longer near the peak of his powers, he had even less leverage than in off-seasons past. The Yanks offered for him to coach their minor league affiliate, the Newark Bears, but Babe saw it as a demotion and refused. While he had long maintained that he would retire after the 1933 season, his 20th in the bigs, Babe returned to the diamond in 1934.

It was hard to watch. While he was still an occasional threat at the plate with 22 home runs, Ruth struggled to round the bases and was a flat-out liability in the outfield. He seldom had the stamina to play a full nine innings despite

> ## *While he was* still an occasional threat at the plate, Babe struggled."

rarely running all that much, but he refused to be relegated to merely a pinch-hitting role. When he made a him-or-me ultimatum to management after the season regarding McCarthy, it was an easy choice for the Yankees brass to make. By the time Babe returned to American soil after an off-season barnstorming trip in Japan, the Yanks had found a place to send him where, ostensibly, he would get a chance to coach.

Babe was the center of attention at the Polo Grounds for the 1944 All-American Boys' Baseball Game, which featured 16- and 17-year-old players, representing 29 of the 48 states.

STAR POWER
Babe, here with Gary Cooper (left) played himself in the 1942 classic Lou Gehrig biopic, *The Pride of the Yankees*. The former slugger reportedly lost over 47 pounds so he could look more like his playing days.

> "
> *New York sent*
> Babe's rights to the Braves
> for nothing, except to get
> his salary off their books."

Judge Emil Fuchs, owner of the National League's Boston Braves, had long had his sights set on acquiring the Bambino, and finally the time was right. New York sent Babe's rights to Fuchs for nothing in exchange, simply happy to get his salary off their books. The slugger accepted the deal on the condition that he would be a player–coach. Fuchs suggested that, after a season as an assistant to manager Bill McKechnie, Babe would become the Brave's manager, with McKechnie moving to the team's front office. Babe signed for $25,000, and he also expected to rake in profits from team stock that Fuchs convinced him to buy.

None of Fuchs' pseudo-promises came to bear. Taking himself in and out of the lineup was the extent of Babe's coaching duties, and the team was far from making a profit. To be fair, Babe fell far short of delivering on his end of the bargain as the team's highest-paid player. While there were some highlights, including a three-homer game in Pittsburgh on May 25, he batted only .181 over 28 games, playing his last-ever game in the majors in the first

ON THE SIDELINES
In June of 1938, Ruth signed on as a coach for the Brooklyn Dodgers, who wanted him to take batting practice before games to draw fans. But a feud with Dodgers' captain Leo Durocher, dating back to their days as Yankee teammates, contributed to Babe's ouster at the end of the season.

leg of a doubleheader in Philadelphia on May 30, 1935. Days later, Fuchs released him from the team. Babe Ruth was done as a professional ballplayer.

Like many athletes who had dedicated their entire lives to a single sport, Babe struggled to find fulfillment once the game was done with him. He golfed so frequently at St. Albans Country Club in Queens, New York, that Claire would often phone the clubhouse in the evening telling him to get home to their Manhattan apartment.

Although Babe rarely went to the ballpark, he was in attendance at the iconic Lou Gehrig Appreciation Day at Yankee Stadium on July 4, 1939. Two weeks earlier, Gehrig had been diagnosed with ALS, and he gave an improvised speech that brought the crowd to tears. "I may have had a tough break, but I have an awful lot to live for," Gehrig concluded. Babe and Lou embraced, effectively ending a petty feud the two had upheld since 1934. Gehrig died two years later, in June 1941.

That same year, Babe's recurring health issues worsened. He was twice hospitalized in 1941 but never diagnosed with anything beyond exhaustion. By 1946, his health troubles had grown far more serious. A tumor wrapped around the carotid artery on the left side of his neck, and he was hospitalized for three months. Realizing the severity of Babe's state, Commissioner of Baseball A.B. Chandler declared April 27 Babe Ruth Day. The festivities called to mind Gehrig's bittersweet affair from years earlier, as 60,000 fans at Yankee Stadium watched Babe give an emotional speech.

BABE RUTH'S LIFE IN PICTURES | 145

Photographer Nat Fein captured Babe's last appearance in Yankee Stadium with this Pulitzer Prize-winning photo, taken on June 13, 1948. Two months later, Ruth succumbed to cancer.

DEATH OF AN ICON
After Babe passed away on August 16, 1948, his casket was displayed in the rotunda of Yankee Stadium for two days. An estimated 77,000 people passed through to pay their respects to the Sultan of Swat.

> **"** *Realizing the* severity of Babe's state, Commissioner of Baseball A.B. Chandler declared April 27, 1947, Babe Ruth Day.**"**

Although he didn't know it until near the end, Babe had cancer. He was given treatments like X-ray therapies, surgery to remove the tumor that was protruding from the base of his skull, and even early chemotherapy.

Babe attended the 25th anniversary celebration of Yankee Stadium in June of 1948, but needed to use a baseball bat as a cane to walk out onto the field when his name was called over the speakers. As always, the cheers were enormous. Two months later, Babe passed away at Manhattan's Memorial Hospital. He was 53 years old.

Over the last few days of his life, thousands stood vigil outside the hospital. When his open casket was displayed for two days in the Yankee Stadium rotunda, 77,000 came to pay their respects. During his funeral at St. Patrick's Cathedral, a crowd of 75,000 stood silent outside the church. Even in death, Babe Ruth was larger than life. ◆

12

A LASTING LEGACY

In the near-century that has passed since Babe Ruth dominated baseball, he remains one of the greatest to ever play the game. From the field at Yankee Stadium to the records he still holds, there's much to be said about the man who made the sport America's pastime.

Thousands of fans lined up to see Babe Ruth play—he was easily the New York Yankees' greatest draw. "I just try my best," he once said. "And sometimes I connect squarely."

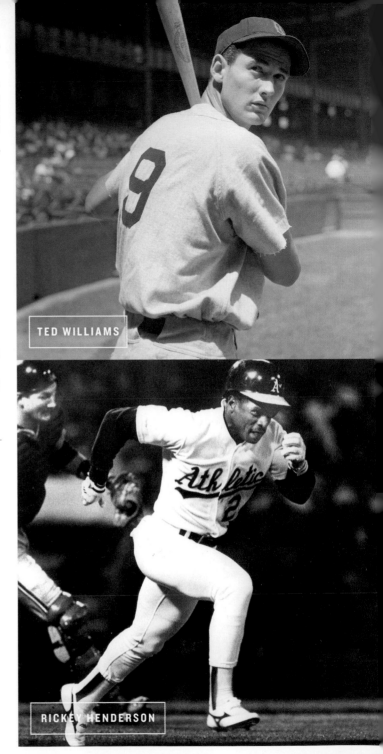

MAKING HISTORY
Many top players have chased Ruth's records in the decades since the great Bambino set them, but a few outstanding achievements still remain today. (See page 164.)

The RECORD BREAKERS

TED WILLIAMS

RICKEY HENDERSON

Few, if any, players in baseball history have a statistical résumé that is as impressive as Babe Ruth's. But perhaps an even better testament to his greatness than his many records is the list of All-Star athletes who broke them— a collection of some of the game's most important icons. Consider how these fellow legends dominated their own time on the field.

ROGER MARIS

HANK AARON

BARRY BONDS

BABE RUTH

Ted Williams

BABE'S RECORD BROKEN

Career On-Base Percentage (OBP):
.4817 (1939–42; 1946–60)

While an at-bat can have many outcomes, one simple question usually reveals whether it had a positive outcome: Did the batter get on base? On-base percentage (OBP) tells us how often the answer is "yes" for a given player. It's a simple, effective measure of success.

Babe Ruth retired with a .473 career OBP, better than any player who came before him. And it's a number that's only been surpassed once in the decades since. But it actually didn't take all that long for the record to fall: Babe's on-base bona fides were bested by Ted Williams, whose career started in 1939, a mere four years after Babe's ended.

Known as Teddy Ballgame, Williams also began his time in the pros with the Boston Red Sox. But unlike the Babe, Williams never played anywhere else. He joined the Sox at the age of 20 and retired as a member of the ballclub after the 1960 season, at 42. In that time, he built one of the finest careers that baseball has ever seen. Williams was a 19-time American League All-Star, a six-time bat-

ting champion, a two-time Triple Crown winner, and a two-time MVP. He batted .406 in 1941, making him the last player to ever hit .400 in a season.

Williams had 2,654 hits in his career (77th of all time), 521 home runs (20th) and 1,839 RBIs (15th), but volume stats don't capture his greatness. Like many players of his generation, Williams was drafted during World War II. He missed the 1943, '44 and '45 seasons serving in the Navy and Marine Corps, and also missed time years later to go on active duty in the Korean War. His military service, along with his baseball heroics and charity, earned him the Presidential Medal of Freedom in 1991.

In a 1943 charity game at Fenway Park, Williams played on a military All-Star team managed by none other than Babe Ruth. "Hiya, kid. You remind me a lot of myself. I love to hit," Babe said to Williams when the two were first introduced. "You're one of the most natural ballplayers I've ever seen. And if my record is broken, I hope you're the one to do it."

While Babe was referring to his more celebrated home run record, the all-time OBP crown that Williams claimed instead is one that feels more fitting, a tribute to his well-roundedness as a batter. "Fifty percent of hitting is above the shoulders," Williams once said, a statement that reflected his meticulous, patient approach at the plate. But he also understood that baseball was a game and considered himself lucky to be a part of it, quipping, "I've found that you don't need to wear a necktie if you can hit."

Roger Maris

BABE'S RECORD BROKEN

Single-Season Home Runs: 61 (1961)

When described broadly, Roger Maris' pursuit and capture of Babe Ruth's single-season home run record in 1961 has a storybook appeal: two Yankee outfielders—Maris and Mickey Mantle, chasing Babe's record all summer, with Maris ultimately hitting the record-breaker in Yankee Stadium. Plus, the Yanks went on to win the World Series. Could Babe's record have been broken in a more perfect fashion? Yes—or at least, many New Yorkers seemed to think so.

Raised in North Dakota, Maris played three promising seasons in the big leagues before donning the pinstripes in 1960. Immediately, his career took off: He won the MVP that very first year in New York, and the Yankees improved their record by 18 wins from the previous season. But even that tremendous 39-home run campaign paled in comparison to what would come next for Maris.

The American League expanded its schedule from 154 games to 162 before the 1961 season, prompting a reporter to ask Maris if the additional at-bats might help someone break Babe's home run record. "No one's touching it," Roger responded. But Maris and Mantle started hot and stayed hot, and it quickly became clear that, in fact, both of the "M&M Boys" had a real shot to top 60 homers.

While that should have made for a fun summer, New York media has a way of finding controversy. Local columnists built up a Maris-Mantle rivalry, a narrative that seems to have had very little basis in fact. Fans bought into it and sided nearly unanimously with The Mick, who'd been a beloved superstar in the Bronx for a full decade at that point.

The media also made a fuss about whether a home run record set in a 162-game season could be considered legitimate. The concern became so widespread that baseball commissioner Ford Frick announced that if such a record were set after Game 154, it would be accompanied by an asterisk.

Maris was occasionally booed by Yankees fans defensive of Mantle or of Ruth's record. He was assigned an NYPD officer as security after receiving death threats. He suffered from anxiety as a result, occasionally losing clumps of hair at a time.

But the negativity didn't slow him down. Mantle missed the final stretch of the regular season with an injury, leaving Maris in the clear to take down the record alone. He hit No. 61 on October 1 against the Red Sox, the 162nd and final game of the year. The record has since been surpassed six times, but Roger's 61-homer season still ranks seventh of all time—and without an asterisk.

Hank Aaron

BABE'S RECORD BROKEN
Career Home Runs: 755 (1954–76)

As a young Black ballplayer in Alabama, Hank Aaron grew up idolizing Jackie Robinson. As for Babe? "For years, the only way I related to him was as the guy with the big stomach," Aaron said. "I didn't think any more about him."

But baseball has a way of connecting greats across eras and Aaron, like Ruth, was one of the greatest to ever do it. After a brief stint in the Negro Leagues, Aaron signed with the Milwaukee Braves and started with the big league club in 1954. He was an impact player right away, and was named an All-Star for the first of 21 times in his career in his second season. In 1957, he won the MVP and homered three times in seven games to lead the Braves to a World Series victory over the Yankees. In 1963, he became the third player (after Ken Williams and Willie Mays) to hit 30 homers and steal 30 bases in a single season. In 1968, he became the first player for the Braves—who had relocated to Atlanta by that time—to reach 500 career home runs. In 1970, he notched his 3,000th hit.

Aaron was so good for so long, hitting 30-plus home runs in 15 different seasons, that he finished the 1973 season at 39 years old with 713 career home runs—one shy of Ruth. He received hundreds of thousands of letters from fans over the summer, much of it admiring. But like his idol Robinson, he also quietly endured vicious racism: No small number of letters contained hate speech, slurs and even death threats.

On the first pitch he faced in the 1974 season, Hammerin' Hank hit No. 714 in Cincinnati. Four days later, in front of a record crowd in Atlanta, Aaron hit the record breaker against Los Angeles. Dodgers broadcaster Vin Scully summed up the significance of the moment perfectly.

"What a marvelous moment for baseball, what a marvelous moment for Atlanta and the state of Georgia, what a marvelous moment for the country and the world," Scully exclaimed. "A Black man is getting a standing ovation in the Deep South for breaking a record of an all-time baseball idol."

Aaron finished his career with 755 home runs, a record that stood for 31 years and a total that may never be topped again. To this day, he remains the all-time king of runs batted in (2,297), total bases (6,856) and extra-base hits (1,477). The records are testaments to Aaron's unparalleled sustained excellence, and his refusal to give in to obstacles.

"My motto was to always keep swinging," he once said. "Whether I was in a slump or feeling badly or having trouble off the field, the only thing to do was keep swinging."

Rickey Henderson

BABE'S RECORD BROKEN

Career Walks: 2,190 (1979–2003)

Rickey Henderson is major league baseball's all-time leader in career steals. You've seen enough photos of Babe Ruth to know that's not the Ruth record that Henderson broke. But consider what it means about Henderson. While he hit the occasional home run—and in fact holds the MLB record for most career leadoff home runs—he was not a menacing power hitter in the mold of Babe. So the last thing any pitcher would want to do while pitching to Rickey would be to walk him, issuing him a free pass to first, and a license to tear up the base paths.

And yet Rickey walked. A lot: 2,190 times—enough to break Babe's record 2,062 bases on balls. The record breaker came in San Diego on April 25, 2001, when Henderson was a member of the Padres. After the game, he sounded ahead of his time in recognizing the significance of his own achievement. "Walks have been a lot underappreciated," he said. "It's lost in the stat sheets. It lost its appeal somewhere. Another thing lost in the stats is on-base percentage. That's the most important thing in baseball. If nobody's on base, nobody scores."

Widely regarded as the best leadoff hitter in the history of the game, Henderson took 796 of his walks to start off an inning. Those free passes often resulted in what came to be known as a Rickey Run: a walk and steal by Henderson, an infield out and a sacrifice fly—all translating into a run scored without a single hit.

While the walks record was later broken by Barry Bonds, Henderson still holds the major league records for career runs (2,295) and single-season steals (130 in 1982), in addition to his aforementioned records for career steals (1,406) and leadoff homers (81). As he tells it, it's the runs record that means the most. "The No. 1 record in baseball is runs scored," he once said, back before he had taken the crown as his own. "Everything else I've done has been toward scoring runs."

In addition to his historic on-field accomplishments, Henderson was one of the game's biggest personalities. He once proudly framed and displayed his check for a $1 million signing bonus instead of cashing it. He frequently referred to himself in the third person; one story places him naked in front of a mirror, reciting a pregame mantra of "Rickey's the best." While never confirmed, it's certainly in line with Henderson's public persona.

Henderson played in the majors until he was 44, and even played for a couple years after that in Independent Leagues. Like Babe, his dedication to, and love of, the game played a large role in his greatness.

BREAKING AWAY
"It's a wonderful honor," Bonds said
after hitting home run No. 715 in May 2006.
"Hank Aaron is the home run king and I won't
disrespect that ever.... I have a lot of respect
for Babe Ruth and what he's done."

Barry Bonds

BABE'S RECORDS BROKEN

Single-Season Home Runs: 73 (2001)

Single-Season Slugging Percentage:
.863 (2001)

Single-Season Walks: 177 (2001)

On-Base Plus Slugging Percentage:
1.381 (2002)

Career Home Runs: 762 (1986–2007)

By the time Barry Bonds was climbing to the top of the all-time home run leaderboard, it had been decades since Hank Aaron surpassed Babe Ruth for the top spot on that list. Nonetheless, it was Babe that Bonds had his eyes on.

"Willie's number is always the one that I've strived for," Bonds said in 2003, referencing his godfather Willie Mays' 660 career homers. "And if it does happen, the only number I care about is Babe Ruth's. Because as a left-handed hitter, I wiped him out. That's it. And in the baseball world, Babe Ruth's everything, right? I got his slugging percentage and I'll take his home runs and that's it. Don't talk about him no more."

Bonds' bold words weren't received too kindly. "To suggest that those feats are somehow capable of 'wiping out' Ruth illustrates a complete disregard for the history and tradition of our national game, and its greatest player and star," read a statement from the Babe Ruth Birthplace and Museum.

While minor, that controversy was a microcosm of Bonds' career. He was unapologetically antagonistic, widely disliked by fans of opposing teams—and one of the best to ever pick up a bat.

By 2001, Ruth's single-season home run record had been broken more than once: First by Roger Maris, then multiple times by both Mark McGwire and Sammy Sosa. Bonds joined the elite club with home run No. 60 on September 7, 2001. But he wasn't finished yet—he finished the year with a record-shattering 73 homers. That same year, Bonds also topped two previously unbroken single-season Ruth records: slugging percentage and walks. Babe slugged .847 in 1920, and Bonds slugged .863 81 years later. Today, Ruth and Bonds each own three of the top six slugging seasons of all time. Bonds broke the walks record by drawing 177 free passes, seven more than Ruth took in 1923.

In 2002, Bonds broke Ruth's on-base plus slugging record, posting a 1.381 OPS to best Babe's 1.379 from 1920. He also broke his own walk record (198). Then in 2004, he topped himself in OPS (1.422) and broke the walk record for a third and final time with a staggering 232. By the time he was finished, Bonds had passed Ruth and Aaron with 762 home runs. He remains the all-time leader.

RECORDS BABE STILL HOLDS

The baseball legend continues to stand tall in the record books with some outstanding achievements.

When you've been out of the game for nearly a century, some of your accomplishments are going to be bested—even if you are the Sultan of Swat. Yet incredibly, Babe Ruth is still the sole holder of many of baseball's current records. And in the public eye, he remains for the most part the most popular baseball player to have ever taken the field. As ESPN pronounced in its most recent "Hall of 100" rankings, "There is no doubt that the Babe was the greatest player who ever lived."

To date, here are some of Babe's most noteworthy stats, along with those who have come closest to catching him.

SINGLE-SEASON RECORDS

EXTRA-BASE HITS
1. Babe Ruth: 119 (1921)
2. Lou Gehrig: 117 (1927)
3. Barry Bonds: 107 (2001)
   Chuck Klein: 107 (1930)
5. Todd Helton: 105 (2001)

TOTAL BASES
1. Babe Ruth: 457 (1921)
2. Rogers Hornsby: 450 (1922)
3. Lou Gehrig: 447 (1927)
4. Chuck Klein: 445 (1930)
5. Jimmie Foxx: 438 (1932)

CAREER RECORDS

SLUGGING PERCENTAGE
1. Babe Ruth: .690
2. Ted Williams: .634
3. Lou Gehrig: .632
4. Jimmie Foxx: .609
5. Barry Bonds: .607

ON-BASE PLUS SLUGGING PERCENTAGE
1. Babe Ruth: 1.164
2. Ted Williams: 1.116
3. Lou Gehrig: 1.080
4. Barry Bonds: 1.051
5. Jimmie Foxx: 1.038

MOST HOME RUN CROWNS
1. Babe Ruth: 12
2. Mike Schmidt: 8
3. Ralph Kiner: 7
4. Gavvy Cravath: 6
   Harmon Killebrew: 6
   Mel Ott: 6

MOST MULTI-HOME RUN GAMES
1 Babe Ruth: 72
2. Barry Bonds: 71
3. Sammy Sosa: 69
4. Mark McGwire: 67
5. Hank Aaron: 62

A LASTING LEGACY

HOME FIELD
The original dimensions at
Yankee Stadium were 295 feet
(right field), 281 feet (left field)
and 490 feet (center field,
aka "Death Valley").

The
HOUSE
THAT RUTH
BUILT

Opened in 1923, the stadium on
East 161st Street and River Avenue
in the Bronx was home to many
of baseball's greatest players,
teams and personalities. While
the original Yankee Stadium
finally gave way to a successor in
2009, the moments and memories
it hosted will stand the test of
time, from World Series magic
to the wonder of rock 'n' roll.
Here are just a few of them.

Larsen Pitches a Perfect World Series Game

OCTOBER 8, 1956
Yankees 2, Dodgers 0

While a solid contributor to the pennant-winning 1956 Yankees, starting pitcher Don Larsen was far from its ace, finishing fourth on the pitching staff in wins. In Game 2 of the World Series at Ebbets Field against the Brooklyn Dodgers, Larsen lasted only 1⅔ innings, surrendering four runs in a Yankees loss. When Larsen took the mound again for Game 5, the series was tied 2–2. No one foresaw what happened next.

In only 97 pitches, Larsen threw a perfect game—the only perfect game in postseason history, let alone the World Series, to this day. Only once, in the first inning, did a batter get to a three-ball count. And the Dodgers lineup was formidable, with stars like Duke Snider, Gil Hodges and Jackie Robinson.

When Larsen struck out the final batter to end the game, catcher Yogi Berra and the rest of the Yankees swarmed their pitcher. "I was so nervous I couldn't think straight," Larsen said of the game's later innings. "Yogi had to do my thinking for me."

The Greatest (Football) Game Ever Played

DECEMBER 28, 1958

Colts 23, Giants 17 (OT)

For its 85 years in use, the original Yankee Stadium was primarily known for baseball. But long-time New York sports fans will recall that the Bronx Bombers' home also hosted the New York Giants from 1956 to 1973.

Only two years removed from winning a championship, the 1958 Giants made another run at the title. Thanks to a league-best defense and a many-headed rushing attack that included the legendary Frank Gifford, New York finished 9–3 in the regular season. After dismantling the Cleveland Browns 10–0 in the playoffs, they prepared to host the Baltimore Colts in the championship game.

It was a rollicking, back-and-forth affair. The Colts led 14–3 at half, the Giants stormed back to lead 17–14 late in the fourth quarter, and the Colts kicked a field goal with seven seconds left to send the game to overtime—the first extra period in NFL playoff history. Colts quarterback Johnny Unitas led his team on a 13-play game-winning drive, with running back Alan Ameche scoring the sudden-death game-winner.

Dubbed "The Greatest Game Ever Played," the contest is credited with jump-starting football's rise in popularity. And while a bitter loss for New York, fans couldn't complain too much—the Yanks had just won the World Series two months earlier.

HEADING FOR HOME
So many fans rushed the field after Chambliss'
dinger that he wasn't sure he had actually tagged all
the bases. After going to the clubhouse, he returned
to the field (disguised in a police raincoat) and
touched the hole where home plate had once been.

Chris Chambliss Walks It Off

OCTOBER 14, 1976

Yankees 7, Royals 6

While trips to the postseason are generally considered business as usual for the New York Yankees, that wasn't the case for the 1976 team. It had been 12 years since the franchise last went to the playoffs, so when the '76 Yanks won an AL-best 97 games to earn a spot in the American League Championship Series, they were determined to take advantage.

The series against the Kansas City Royals was a nail-biter; each team won two of the first four games to force a decisive Game 5 at Yankee Stadium. After a tight first few innings, New York took a three-run lead in the sixth thanks in part to a throwing error by star KC third baseman George Brett. Brett, however, made up for it, tying the game with a three-run bomb in the eighth.

Leading off in the bottom of the ninth for the Yankees was first baseman Chris Chambliss, who had received his only career All-Star nod earlier that season. On Royals reliever Mark Littrell's very first pitch, Chambliss crushed a home run to right-center field. Before it even hit the ground, Yankees fans rushed the field.

"I remember tripping—I went down to one knee," Chambliss recalled years later. "Somebody tried to steal my helmet from behind. From then on it was like, 'How do I get myself to the dugout?'"

While the Yankees would go on to be swept in the World Series by the Cincinnati Reds, they won the next two World Series after that (against the Los Angeles Dodgers in both 1977 and 1978)— again defeating the Royals in the ALCS each time.

Three Homers for Mr. October

OCTOBER 18, 1977

Yankees 8, Dodgers 4

A month after losing the 1976 World Series, the Yankees made a big-ticket acquisition in signing perennial All-Star outfielder Reggie Jackson. Jackson immediately provided a strong return on investment for New York, hitting 32 home runs and getting 110 RBIs in his first season with the club. But he also had a noticeably strong personality, resulting in a few incidents with more tenured Yankees—including a physical altercation in the dugout with manager Billy Martin.

But Jackson was known for playoff prowess, so by the postseason all was forgiven. Star Yankee catcher Thurman Munson even gave Jackson the nickname "Mr. October," albeit perhaps somewhat facetiously.

After taking down the Royals in five games, New York advanced to a World Series showdown with the Los Angeles Dodgers. Mr. October had hit only .125 in the ALCS, but he came alive in the Fall Classic, notching six hits and two home runs in the first five games of the series to help New York take a 3–2 lead.

But Jackson was just getting started. In the fourth inning of Game 6, he launched a line drive into the right field stands to put the Yankees up 4–3. The next inning he hit another one, making the lead 5–3. The cherry on top came in the eighth, as Jackson hit a staggering 475-foot bomb to center field to put the Yanks up 8–3, all but cementing their 21st World Series championship.

"Oh, what a beam on his face," announcer Howard Cosell yelled as Jackson crossed home plate. "Who can blame him? He's answered the whole world!"

PIANO MAN
"It was 52 years ago on June 22 in this stadium that Joe Louis knocked out Max Schmeling!" Billy Joel told the sold-out crowd soon after he took the stage for his own thrilling performance.

THREE TIMES THE CHARM
David Cone (opposite page) was not the first Yankee since Don Larsen to throw a perfect game at home: One year earlier, on May 17, 1998, David Wells retired all 27 hitters he faced on the Minnesota Twins.

Billy Joel Starts the Fire

JUNE 22–23, 1990
Friday, June 22–SOLD OUT
Saturday, June 23–SOLD OUT

Billy Joel wasn't the first to perform a concert at Yankee Stadium. A-list acts such as Ray Charles, Stevie Wonder and The Beach Boys all preceded him. But when Joel took the stage in the outfield in June 1990, it was a distinctly New York moment.

Born in the Bronx and raised on Long Island, Joel dropped out of high school to pursue music. He released some of the most popular music of the '70s and '80s—albums like *The Stranger* and *Glass Houses*, and hit singles such as "Only the Good Die Young," "Uptown Girl" and "We Didn't Start the Fire."

To no one's surprise, Joel pulled out all the stops for his Yankee Stadium shows, giving the crowd his best-known upbeat pop hits, tender ballads and rock 'n' roll jams. One highlight was when Joel put on a Yankees cap before tearing through "Big Shot," ending the song with some improvised gymnastics on top of his piano. It was a display of pure New York swagger that would've left even Babe Ruth impressed.

David Cone's Perfect Game

JULY 18, 1999

Yankees 6, Expos 0

On Yogi Berra Day, New York celebrated one of the greatest to ever wear pinstripes. A three-time MVP who won 12 World Series with the Yankees as a player and coach, Berra was one of baseball's all-time best characters. As part of the ceremony, Berra caught the first pitch from Don Larsen, whose perfect game he caught in the 1956 World Series. "Perfect, it's absolutely perfect, and it has been a perfect day today," said Yankees TV announcer Bobby Murcer as the old teammates walked off the field.

On the mound for the game that followed was David Cone, a key member of New York's 1996 and 1998 championship teams. It was 95 degrees on the field, but Cone, who'd suffered an aneurysm two years earlier, always seemed to pitch better in the heat after the incident. With Larsen watching, Cone miraculously tossed a perfect game of his own, striking out 10 Montreal Expos on 88 pitches. Like Larsen—and each of the other few pitchers to ever throw a perfecto—Cone was swarmed by his teammates after the 27th out. The Yanks would go on to beat the Braves in the World Series that year, with Cone earning a dominant win in Game 2. "What an honor," Cone said after the game. "All the Yankee legends here. Don Larsen in the park. Yogi Berra Day. It makes you stop and think about the Yankee magic and the mystique of this ballpark."

PRESIDENTIAL PRESENCE
Before heading up to the Bronx, President Bush visited the first responders who were still working amid the rubble at the World Trade Center. On the field, he wore a bulletproof vest under his FDNY jacket.

President Bush Throws a Strike

OCTOBER 30, 2001

Yankees 2, Diamondbacks 1

After the September 11, 2001, terrorist attacks on the United States, major league baseball canceled all games for the next week. In a devastated New York City, Yankees including Derek Jeter, Bernie Williams and manager Joe Torre took action, visiting first responders, victims and families to provide what small measure of comfort they could.

When baseball returned, competition took a back seat to what the game stood for: a resilient, united America. Instead of their usual caps, the Yankees and New York Mets wore NYPD and FDNY caps. In the Mets' first game back in Queens, star catcher Mike Piazza hit a dramatic game-winning home run.

Instead of their usual role as villains, the Yankees had all of America behind them during their 2001 playoff run. They survived a 0–2 deficit in the ALDS to beat the Athletics, and vanquished the 116-win Seattle Mariners in a five-game ALCS, advancing to face the Diamondbacks in the World Series.

The series opened in Arizona before shifting to the Bronx for Game 3, where President George W. Bush would throw the ceremonial first pitch. In the World Series at Yankee Stadium, just weeks after 9/11, it was unquestionably the most important presidential first pitch in baseball history. Before President Bush took the mound, Jeter reminded him of the stakes. "Don't bounce it—they'll boo you," Jeter half-joked.

President Bush threw a perfect strike.

"I had never had such an adrenaline rush as when I finally made it to the mound," said President Bush. "I was saying to the crowd, 'I'm with you, the country's with you.'... I've never felt anything so powerful and emotions so strong, and the collective will of the crowd so evident."

OFTEN OUTSHADOWED
"I always knew that as long as I was following Babe to the plate I could have gone up there and stood on my head. No one would have noticed the difference," Lou Gehrig famously said of his teammate and onetime friend.

From THE BABE'S MOUTH

"Baseball was, is and always will be to me the best game in the world."

———

"IF I'D TRIED FOR THEM DINKY SINGLES I COULD'VE BATTED AROUND .600."

———

"I HAVE JUST ONE SUPERSTITION. Whenever I hit a home run, I make certain I touch all four bases."

"

The way a team plays as a whole determines its success. You may have the greatest bunch of individual stars in the world, but if they don't play together, the club won't be worth a dime."

———

"I LEARNED EARLY TO DRINK BEER, WINE AND WHISKEY. AND I THINK I WAS ABOUT 5 WHEN I FIRST CHEWED TOBACCO."

"All I can tell them is pick a good one and sock it. I get back to the dugout and they ask me what pitch I hit and I tell them I don't know except it looked good."

Reading isn't good for a ballplayer. Not good for his eyes. If my eyes went bad even a little bit I couldn't hit home runs. So I gave up reading."

"IF IT WASN'T FOR BASEBALL, I'd be in either the penitentiary or the cemetery."

"Yesterday's home runs don't win today's games."

"I won't be happy until we have every boy in America between the ages of 6 and 16 wearing a glove and swinging a bat."

Gee, it's lonesome in the outfield. It's hard to keep awake with nothing to do."

"ALL BALLPLAYERS SHOULD QUIT WHEN IT STARTS TO FEEL AS IF ALL THE BASELINES RUN UPHILL."

"Don't ever forget two things I'm going to tell you. One, don't believe everything that's written about you. Two, don't pick up too many checks."

How
THE WORLD SAW HIM

"Some 20 years ago I stopped talking about the Babe for the simple reason that I realized that those who had never seen him didn't believe me." —Tommy Holmes, *sportswriter*

"EVERY BIG LEAGUER AND HIS WIFE SHOULD TEACH THEIR CHILDREN TO PRAY, 'GOD BLESS MOMMY, GOD BLESS DADDY, AND GOD BLESS BABE RUTH.'" —WAITE HOYT, TEAMMATE

"To understand him you had to understand this: He wasn't human."
—Joe Dugan, teammate

"
Babe Ruth is the greatest baseball player that ever lived. People say he was less than a god but more than a man. You know, like Hercules or something."
—Benny, *The Sandlot*

**"THERE WILL NEVER BE ANOTHER BABE RUTH. HE WAS THE GREATEST HOME RUN HITTER WHO EVER LIVED. THEY NAMED A CANDY BAR AFTER HIM."
—REGGIE JACKSON, HALL OF FAME BATTER**

"No one hit home runs the way Babe did. They were something special. They were like homing pigeons. The ball would leave the bat, pause briefly, suddenly gain its bearings, then take off for the stands." —Dizzy Dean, Hall of Fame pitcher

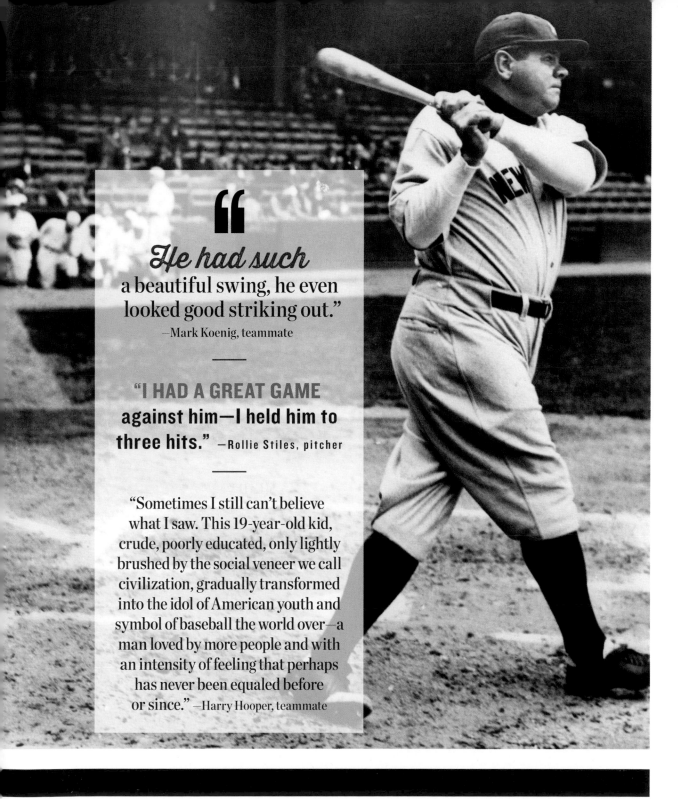

"

He had such a beautiful swing, he even looked good striking out."
—Mark Koenig, teammate

"I HAD A GREAT GAME against him—I held him to three hits." —Rollie Stiles, pitcher

"Sometimes I still can't believe what I saw. This 19-year-old kid, crude, poorly educated, only lightly brushed by the social veneer we call civilization, gradually transformed into the idol of American youth and symbol of baseball the world over—a man loved by more people and with an intensity of feeling that perhaps has never been equaled before or since." —Harry Hooper, teammate

FINAL FAREWELL

On April 27, 1947, a crowd of 58,339 gathered at Yankee Stadium for Babe Ruth Day to honor the legend, who at age 53 was in the late stages of his battle with nasopharyngeal cancer. The ceremony was transmitted throughout the world. As *The New York Times* reported, "Just before he spoke, Ruth started to cough and it appeared that he might break down because of the thunderous cheers that came his way. But once he started to talk, he was all right, still the champion. It was the many men who surrounded him on the field, players, newspaper and radio persons, who choked up."

Here's what the Babe had to say:

"Thank you very much, ladies and gentlemen. You know how bad my voice sounds. Well, it feels just as bad.

"You know, this baseball game of ours comes up from the youth. That means the boys. And after you're a boy and grow up to play ball, then you come to the boys you see representing clubs today in your national pastime. The only real game in the world, I think, is baseball. As a rule, people think that if you give boys a football or a baseball or something like that, they naturally become athletes right away. But you can't do that in baseball. You got to start from way down, at the bottom, when the boys are 6 or 7 years of age. You can't wait until they're 15 or 16. You got to let it grow up with you, if you're the boy. And if you try hard enough, you're bound to come out on top, just as these boys here have come to the top now."

> **" *There have been* so many lovely things said about me today that I'm glad to have had the opportunity to thank everybody. Thank you."**